Military
Musings

The experiences of a Kenya-born English lad
in the fight against the terrorism of
the Mau-Mau Rebellion

Leonard J Gill

Copyright © 2003 by Leonard J. Gill

All rights reserved. No part of this publication may be reproduced, stored in a retrieval system, or transmitted, in any form or by any means, electronic, mechanical, photocopying, recording, or otherwise, without the written prior permission of the author.

Contact the author at: Post Office Box 2141, Glenwood Springs, Colorado, 81602, USA

Email: banner@rof.net

Note for Librarians: a cataloguing record for this book that includes Dewey Classification and US Library of Congress numbers is available from the National Library of Canada. The complete cataloguing record can be obtained from the National Library's online database at: www.nlc-bnc.ca/amicus/index-e.html

ISBN 1-55395-654-0

TRAFFORD

This book was published *on-demand* in cooperation with Trafford Publishing.
On-demand publishing is a unique process and service of making a book available for retail sale to the public taking advantage of on-demand manufacturing and Internet marketing.
On-demand publishing includes promotions, retail sales, manufacturing, order fulfilment, accounting and collecting royalties on behalf of the author.

Suite 6E, 2333 Government St., Victoria, B.C. V8T 4P4, CANADA
Phone   250-383-6864   Toll-free   1-888-232-4444 (Canada & US)
Fax   250-383-6804   E-mail   sales@trafford.com
Web site   www.trafford.com   TRAFFORD PUBLISHING IS A DIVISION OF TRAFFORD HOLDINGS LTD.
Trafford Catalogue #03-0017   www.trafford.com/robots/03-0017.html

10   9   8   7   6   5   4   3

Acknowledgments

My thanks and best regards go to the men I served with and fond memories of those who are no longer with us:

Alphabetically: Dave McCabe*, Roy Stockwell*, Tony Swain, Pat Watson, Willie Young*, and all my loyal African comrades including Ngalu, Kiptanui, Kiprono, Kilonzo, Lokkitulia, and so many others.

Again, I thank artist, Jack Niswanger for his sketches which add so much to my narrative.

*Deceased at time of writing.

Dedication

This sequel to my earlier books, *Rambunctious Reflections* and *Rollicking Recollections*, tells of the period I was engaged in anti-Mau-Mau terrorist activities in Kenya. I told yarns to my dear wife, Kaye. She found interesting and humorous sidelights among tales of horror and conflict. She insisted I write of my experiences and provided assistance and encouragement. I dedicate this book to her.

Table of Contents

Prologue

Page #
1   A Brief Political History of Kenya
8   Map of Kenya

Chapter 1
1   Anti-Mau-Mau Operations commence

Chapter 2
9   The Draft

Chapter 3
13   Training in Southern Rhodesia (Zimbabwe)

Chapter 4
18   The Lari Massacre

Chapter 5
19   We become a team

Chapter 6
34   4th (Uganda) Battalion of the Kings African Rifles

Chapter 7
39   KAR rations and equipment
43   Feuds dealt with by Kikuyu Guards

Chapter 8
45   Political influence
50   Idi Amin

Chapter 9
53   Mau-Mau oaths
66   Fort Essex

67   Kenya Police Air Wing

Chapter 10
72   Remarkable brothers

Chapter 11
75   Davo, a great fighter and teller of tales
80   An apparition visits Mum
81   Back to Davo and cold, wet reality

Chapter 12
84   Man on the Run
88   A Senior Chief takes action

Chapter 13
92   The 3rd (Kenya) Battalion of the Kings African Rifles takes over from the 4th (Uganda) Battalion

Chapter 14
97   Treatment in a British Military Hospital, Nairobi

Chapter 15
106   3rd K.A.R. takes over Fort Essex
110   Lokkitulia learns a lesson
113   A visitor comes to Fort Essex

Chapter 16
116   Some Tribal Traits
118   Overindulgence

Chapter 17
120   Gentlewoman of the Bush

Chapter 18
128   Teamwork generates telepathy

Prologue

A Brief Political History of Kenya

In the latter half of the 19th Century, explorers, hunters and missionaries visited eastern Africa. Prior to that time, Arabs from the Middle East had operated a slave trade for several hundred years. They made their base on the Spice Islands of Zanzibar and Pemba off the coast of what is now Tanzania, from where they could operate in safety. Tanzania was their main source of slaves but, over time, the Arabs operated northward along the coastal strip and collected slaves from what is now Kenya. Uganda was not a popular source of slaves as it was too far from the coast, and there were rumors that the Uganda tribes practiced cannibalism.

The arrival of Europeans slowed and finally put a stop to the slave trade. In 1885 Queen Victoria's Prime Minister, Benjamin Disraeli, voiced the opinion that Britain had a duty to bring civilization and peace to Africa.

The early European visitors to British East Africa (Kenya) had reported that vast areas were unoccupied. Each tribe inhabited land isolated from other tribes, and encroachment towards another's area led to tribal warfare. The cool, upland uninhabited areas, at altitudes between about 7,000 and 10,000 feet above sea level, were to be known as the White Highlands. They were deemed to be ideal for European occupation, and settlement commenced from the beginning of the twentieth century. Native lands were protected by legislation and the colonists were prohibited from purchasing land in the tribal 'reserves'. There was plenty of good land in the White Highlands.

Early British colonial government administrators suggested that the presence of settlers would end tribal warfare, and mitigate the terrible results of famine and disease in humans and livestock. They were to be proved right.

To further encourage white colonization, a railway was built from Mombasa on the coast to Kisumu on Lake Victoria. Building started in 1898 and the single railway line was completed in 1902. Workers had been recruited from India and many elected to stay in Kenya where they formed a body of skilled artisans. Those who settled in the colony brought their families from their homeland and many entered commerce, setting up shops in the towns and villages throughout the colony, even in the most remote areas.

Construction of the railway took the rails across the Athi Plains some 270 miles inland. Hilly country could be seen in the distance, and a shortage of materials led to a stoppage in construction at a place known to the Masai as Nairobi some 300 miles from Mombasa. Perhaps the railroad builders needed to gather themselves for the climb into the hills. Perhaps the siting of Nairobi was, to some extent, similar to the siting of Denver, Colorado where early pioneers stopped to repair wagons, replenish supplies, and gather fresh determination to tackle the mountains. In Kenya the railway builders needed to rest, and since materials were in short supply, the stopping place was determined for them. Tents were erected, kitchens were built, and workshops were set up so that repairs to equipment could be effected. Within a few weeks a town was born. Nairobi was to become the capital of the colony.

In several respects the siting was unfortunate. Deep silt, deposited by the Nairobi River over thousands of years, made building costly. Drainage was a problem. Where there was rock, it was sponge-like with holes filled with silt. Some of these holes, up to twenty feet deep and twenty feet in diameter, were invisible but came to light when building foundations were to be laid. Water was a problem from day one, the Nairobi River being just a small stream. These problems were not evident when Nairobi was little more than a tented camp with a few sheds. When stone buildings were to be constructed requiring permanent drainage and a reliable supply of potable water, the problems became evident. Despite the drawbacks, the town burgeoned and European doctors, dentists, businessmen, industrialists and their families arrived to set up dispensaries, surgeries, shops and workshops. The European population in Kenya was to rise to 55,000 in 1985 when the African population numbered approximately 20 million.

After WWI, there was an influx of settlers from the upper ranks of British society. They were encouraged by government advertisements in Britain to settle in Kenya, a land of opportunity with a superb climate, affordable land, cheap labor, excellent hunting and no taxation. The war had changed life for the upper classes in Britain. Kenya offered a return to a life that had been enjoyed before the war to anyone willing to train workers from the vast unskilled population.

To the south of Nairobi lay the Masai Reserve. To the east, the Wakamba tribe occupied the land. To the west were the hills bordering the White Highlands and to the north lay the Kikuyu Reserve. The settlers quickly found that the Kikuyu were intelligent, hardworking and enthusiastic agriculturists who tilled land similar to much of the White Highlands. The Masai were nomadic cattle owners, uninterested in any other form of occupation. The Wakamba lived in a drier area and practiced agriculture suitable for those conditions.

The settlers employed Kikuyu on farms in the White Highlands, in stores, in their homes as servants, and as assistants to work with Asian artisans in all the skills needed to build European style residences and towns. Of course, people of other tribes also found employment. The proximity of Nairobi to the Kikuyu Reserve and the natural aptitudes and industriousness of the Kikuyu people, together with their numbers, and wide acceptance of British even-handed justice were factors which led to many being employed.

From the earliest days of colonial settlement, the Kikuyu tribe was the most numerous in Kenya. The next largest tribe was the Luo who occupied land around the northeastern area of Lake Victoria. At the beginning of the 20th Century, missionaries estimated the Luo population to number about 66,000. Sixty years later, under British colonial administration, the Luos numbered about 5,000,000. The Kikuyu, starting with a slightly larger population, grew in numbers by a similar factor. The population increase arose from measures introduced under British colonial administration: The cessation of tribal warfare, medical welfare, veterinary services, and forward planning to mitigate famine.

By 1931 the Kikuyu could see that by employing European methods: Mechanization, transportation, brick buildings, warm clothing, medical and veterinary expertise, the rearing of imported livestock and the raising of the wide range of diverse crops, they could themselves develop the White Highlands. Many of them had been employed there as agricultural workers for several years, and had learned the ways of the settlers, and had contributed to adaptation of some European farming methods, crop selection and hybridization of livestock to produce disease resistant strains of animals and cereals.

Kikuyu political unrest had started in 1902. Further political pressure was exerted from 1920 and ten years later a Kikuyu leader, Harry Thuku, was claiming land hunger. He alleged that the White Highlands had been unoccupied only because the tribes had suffered from disease and famine due to crop failure following droughts, their cattle had died from starvation, rinderpest spread by the Cape buffalo, anthrax, east coast fever and rabies carried by wild animals. The reduced population had withdrawn into smaller areas, but the White Highlands were only temporarily abandoned, and much of it actually belonged to the Kikuyu, so it was claimed.

When a Kikuyu man died, all his sons were left an equal portion of his land. If the father owned one acre and had four sons, each inherited a quarter of an acre, which was insufficient to support a family. A man and his wife could till about one acre using hand tools. Many families had more than four sons. Prior to the arrival of Europeans, the Kikuyu merely advanced into unoccupied areas when their population grew. The population numbers waxed and waned with periods of good fortune followed by disease, famine and tribal warfare.

By 1920, Harry Thuku's political platform on the claim of land hunger was taken up by one Kikuyu politician after another. The settlers, supported by the British government, denied the accusation which, in the absence of written records or any evidence of ruins of old villages or past habitation, could not be proved. But some land hungry Kikuyu people were inclined to believe the fiery orations of agitators rather than the logic of the cold measured words of British officials and settlers.

Harry Thuku raised other issues including the right for the Kikuyu to grow coffee, the introduction of a booklet with details of employment, that Africans would be required to carry, and the initiation of tax. These were the stock-in-trade of all African political agitators. Thuku founded the Young Kikuyu Association. In 1930 he was arrested and sent to an isolated area. A riot in Nairobi followed his arrest.

Jomo Kenyatta joined the Young Kikuyu Association in 1922. This was to be superseded by the Kikuyu Central Association (K.C.A.) founded in 1926. Kenyatta was to become the leading Kikuyu politician over the following years. He visited Europe, including Russia, where he stayed for four months and earned himself the reputation of being a Communist. He actually dismissed Communism as an ideology foreign to Kikuyu ways of life. The Kikuyu hold personal assets sacrosanct. Socialism might possibly find acceptance among nomadic people, who regard the territory they occupy as belonging to their tribe, but a Kikuyu man's plot of land and livestock are his.

Kenyatta spread his propaganda through K.C.A.

schools, independent of missionary schools. He imposed oaths of secrecy on members of K.C.A. and denounced soil conservation. This last matter was close to the hearts of land hungry Kikuyu who wanted to farm the land on river edges. This resulted in soil erosion which the Kenya Agricultural Department was trying to stop.

After WW II the Kikuyu Central Association became the Kenya African Union (K.A.U.) in an attempt to broaden the base from a purely Kikuyu tribal association to a national society. The re-vamped organization took over the reins of anti-British activities and began to gain ground and spread disaffection to sister tribes of the Kikuyu in the Embu, Meru and Kamba Reserves. An element of the K.A.U. formed a militant wing that operated under the name of Mau-Mau, which was entirely Kikuyu dominated with a small number of members from other tribes. Their aim was to oust the European settlers and take over their land.

Kenyatta continued to make political progress from 1946 through 1951 despite the formation of non-racial societies founded by settlers who sought to defuse the growing enmity engendered by Kenyatta and his Mau-Mau henchmen. He was a master of evasion, and his speeches were full of equivocation, indicating on the one hand, opposition to crime, but being seditious on the other. His mainly Kikuyu listeners picked out what he really wanted them to hear.

In May 1952, the Mau-Mau murder campaign started. In the following six months fifty-nine loyal Kikuyu had been assassinated. In September of that year, the new Governor, Sir Evelyn Baring, was sworn in. On the 21st October, a State of Emergency was proclaimed and eighty-one Mau-Mau leaders were detained. On the 18th of November Kenyatta and five others were charged with the management of Mau-Mau, a proscribed society. Mau-Mau oathing had been illegal from 1950.

On the 26th November 1952, Tom Mbotela, a former associate of Kenyatta and one-time vice-president of

K.A.U., was murdered by Kenyatta supporters. This was a significant killing as Mbotela was a leader of the Luo tribe who had led his people away from the terrorist movement. The majority of Kenya Africans, including most Kikuyu, were against violence as a means to gain independence from Britain. As in many movements, a small but vociferous element excited unrest among normally peaceful people.

COLONY & PROTECTORATE
OF KENYA 1895-1963

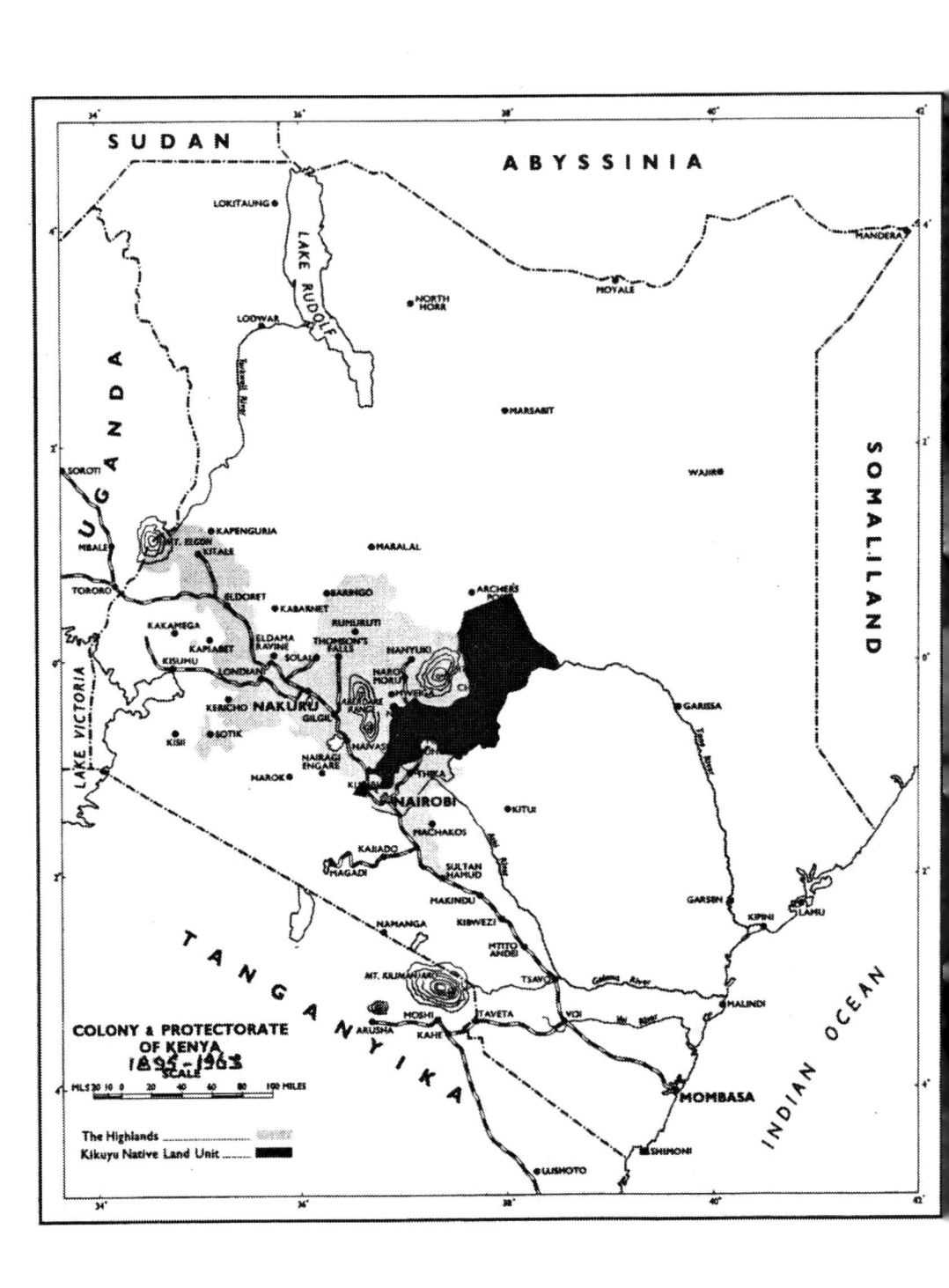

The Highlands
Kikuyu Native Land Unit

1

Anti-Mau-Mau Operations commence

      Meetings, presided over by senior police officers, were held all over the city on the evening of October 20th, 1952. All European able-bodied males over the age of eighteen from every household were required to attend. It was announced the following day an emergency was to be declared by the new governor of Kenya, Sir Evelyn Baring. Along with many other Europeans, I was enrolled into the Kenya Police Reserve. This was to give us certain legal authority, and it was intended that, in due course, we would be required to attend lectures and training when our legal status, responsibilities and the procedures we were to follow would be fully explained.

      Dad was elected Captain of our area, which contained twenty-two homes. I and another Kenya Police Reserve officer were ordered to start patrols that night to inform residents what to expect. There were several houses occupied by women who had not attended the meeting. One house was occupied by a lady who lived alone. As I and my colleague walked across the yard, the gravel crunched under our boots. A window was thrown open and a slim arm, with a Colt .45 semi-automatic pistol in its tiny fist, poked out. BANG!.....BANG!.....BANG! The Colt kicked and sparks flew out of the muzzle until the last shot in the magazine headed for the starlit sky. We then raced the last five yards to the house and flattened ourselves, backs to the wall on either side of the window.

"It's all right," I cried nervously, "it's only us. It's the patrol. We have started patrolling tonight." The arm disappeared.

"I thought you were to start tomorrow night," said a strained female voice.

"Well, we thought we'd start tonight to let everyone know about the routine and what to expect."

"Oh! Well you'd better come in and tell me about it."

We went to the front door and were admitted by a middle-aged, elegant lady wearing a flowing negligee. She had been told by a neighbor something about the plans to protect houses in the area. She offered us a drink and we explained in further detail the scheme that we had been advised to adopt. We swigged our drinks and left to continue our introductory patrol.

Every house was occupied and we were invited in, offered a drink, and asked to disclose the plans that had been made to protect our area. Hours and many drinks later, I and my comrade-in-arms reeled our way homeward thinking that our new duties might be rather fun.

***

We soon settled into a routine patrolling in pairs from 6 p.m. to midnight or midnight to 6 a.m. Dad switched us about so that one didn't always patrol with the same colleague. In this way the best techniques were spread, and the less effective patrollers became more efficient.

There were a few exciting incidents. I was on the 6 p.m. to midnight patrol with a bored partner named Henry Allen, who was inclined to sit down on a culvert and let time pass. We started our shift by strolling around the area for which we were responsible. I carried a .22 rifle loaded with 'shorts'. Henry was more than a little nervous, suspecting I might be trigger happy, and would shoot at anybody or anything. By about 6.30 p.m. the sun was setting, and the curfew had been in force for half an hour. The curfew ruled that all Africans be off the streets by 6 p.m., or face very serious consequences.

Suddenly, I saw an African sneak across the road, and make his way at a crouching run down a wide storm ditch away from us.

"*Simama!* (Stop!)" I yelled. "*Simama!*"

He knew I was shouting at him, as he was no longer crouching, but was sprinting away as fast as he could.

"*Simama!*" I yelled at the top of my voice.

He was now some 80 yards away and running hard. I raised my rifle, took a quick aim and squeezed the trigger. The fugitive stopped. That is to say he fell flat and stayed still. I ran to him with Henry following. As we reached the would-be fugitive, he was struggling to his feet, panting from his exertions and fear. I had shot him in the right buttock, but he was not bleeding much. He was unusually well dressed, and I began to question him. He told us he was a servant from a nearby house. He had had the day off, and had gone to visit a friend across town. On his way back he had been stopped by a police patrol, and taken to the police station for questioning. The police had released him shortly before the curfew hour.

Henry went to his house to get his car, and we took the injured man to his employer, who took him to hospital for treatment. The little slug had not penetrated far, and it was removed quickly, without difficulty. Henry and I were extremely incensed. In releasing the man so close to the curfew hour, the police had put the man's life in danger, as a curfew-breaker could be shot on sight. The following day, Henry and the servant's employer went to lodge a strong complaint at the police station from where the man had been released the previous evening. The attitude amongst the police at the station was one of amusement, but this changed when Henry phoned a senior officer who came immediately to sort things out.

After a short inquiry, I was cleared of any crime. I had acted in accordance with the Emergency Regulations. The servant was back at work in a couple of days, and I went to see him to offer my apologies. He was aware that the policemen who had released him had been reprimanded for endangering his life, and he accepted my apologies.

We had trouble with one or two Europeans who were sympathetic to the political aims of the Mau-Mau. One such individual lived six houses down the road from my parents' house. Mr. Street told my Dad that anyone coming onto his property to carry out an investigation of his servants' quarters would be shot. He was extremely impolite, and sent Dad away with a string of invectives. Dad had seen a large number of Africans hanging around the servants' quarters, and went to the police in our area to ask how he should react to Street's behavior. Dad was fortunate to meet Police Commissioner Hoyle at the station, who gave Dad a bit of confidential advice. Commissioner Hoyle was one of those policemen who, with humor, are usually able to persuade members of the public to be co-operative. Together he and Dad hatched a plan to solve the problem with Mr. Street.

A day or two later, Street went out to his car early in the morning to go to work. He found all four wheels missing, and the car belly down on the gravel. He was furious, and without his car had difficulty in getting to the police station to report the theft. At the Police Station the four wheels were hidden behind the front office counter within inches of where Street stood berating the desk sergeant. The wheels had been delivered by one of Street's neighbors, who had quietly removed them around 4 a.m. that morning. The police officer slowly and meticulously took down details from Street, and then peremptorily dismissed him.

"B - b - b - but aren't you going to *do* anything?" Street stammered furiously.

"Well," answered the policeman calmly, "there's nothing much more we can do."

"Why? What do you mean?" Street spluttered.

"You've threatened to shoot anyone coming onto your property to carry out investigations," replied the policeman.

The outcome was that we were invited to investigate Street's servants' quarters where we found twenty-three people inhabiting quarters built to accommodate five. Several, were taken by the police for further questioning, and the others, except for Street's employees, were sent to their homes in their tribal areas.

After our investigation, the police phoned Street to tell him that his wheels had been recovered, but that he would have to come to collect them as the police didn't operate a delivery service. He had to accompany the collecting vehicle, as he had to sign a receipt for his wheels. He then had the laborious task of jacking his car off the ground to enable him to bolt the wheels back on. Street probably guessed that he had been the victim of a ruse, and didn't ask the police how they had managed to recover the wheels. We had no further trouble from Street, whose antipathy towards his own nationals was a result of our disapproval of his liverish demeanor, a product of excessive alcohol consumption.

My parents' next-door neighbors were Mr. and Mrs. Richardson. They both had foul tempers - a result of the same over-indulgence as Street. Mrs. Richardson could frequently be heard screaming at her servants, who were a moody lot. Richardson had also threatened to harm anyone who set foot on his property, but nobody took him too seriously as it was suspected that, by 2 a.m., both he and his wretched wife would be lying drunk in bed with eyes tight shut and mouths wide open. Dad was informed by the police that they had information to the effect that a Mau-Mau gang leader was holed up in the Richardson's servants' quarters. They asked him to have the situation investigated.

Two butts emerged

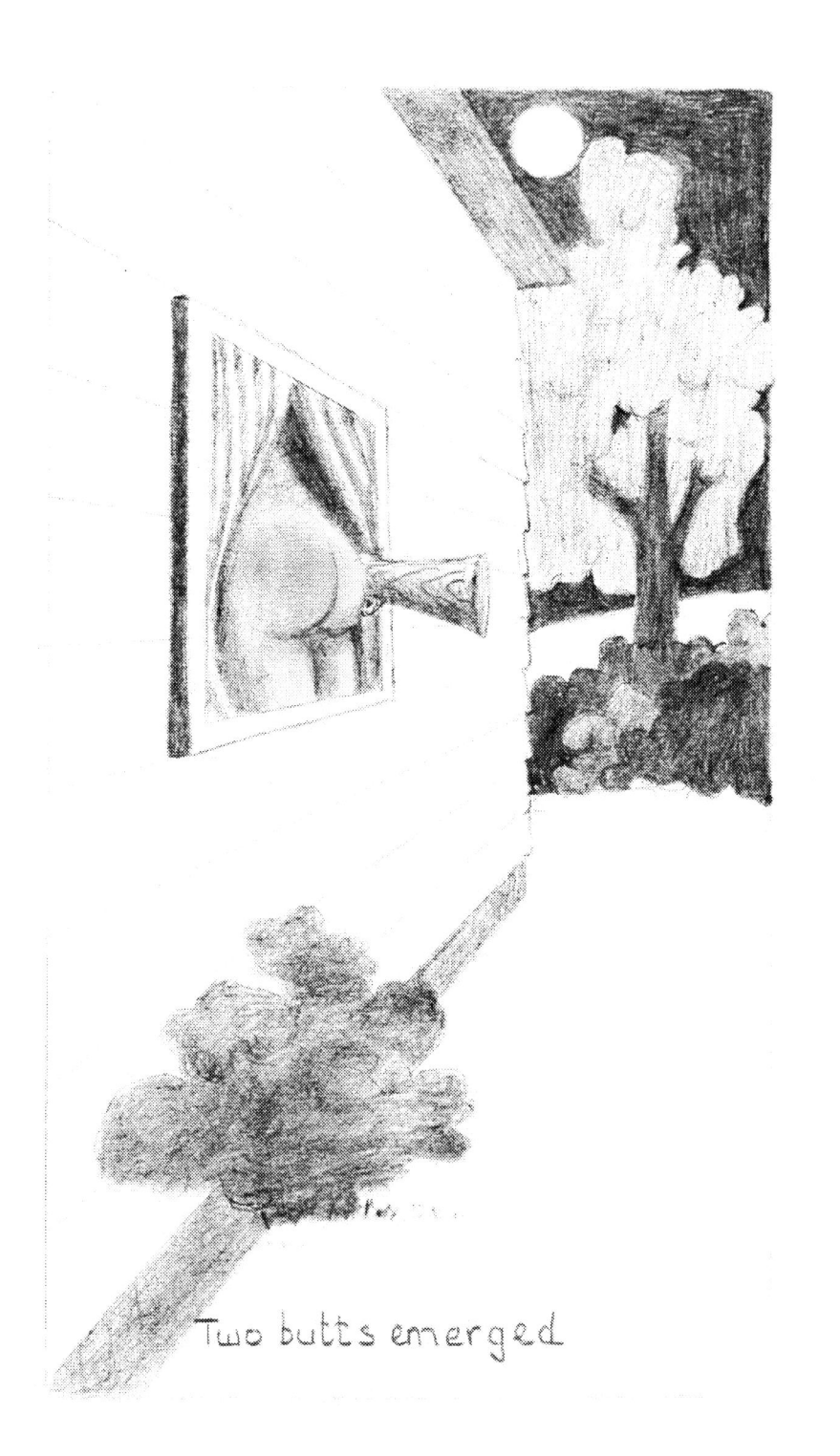

He was warned that the terrorist was possibly armed.

Dad asked me and my patrol colleague for the night, George, to investigate. In moonlight, we approached the servants' quarters stealthily at about 12.30 a.m. I went round to the back while George went to the front door. He hammered loudly, and shouted for everyone to come out. A window two feet from my head was quietly opened, and a moment later a man's bare butt emerged, accompanied by the butt of a rifle. Unaware of my presence, he was trying to make his escape at the furthest point from the front door, where George had called for the occupants to come out.

I fired at the protruding anatomy. The buttocks disappeared, fast. I ran round to assist George, and to warn him that someone in the quarters was armed. The door opened and the occupants surrendered quietly. They came out unarmed. One man was nursing a wounded buttock. I went in and recovered a loaded .275 sporting rifle and fifteen rounds of ammunition.

Dad had not gone to bed, and had heard the shouting and the shot. He phoned the police. Soon there was quite a collection around the quarters. Neither Mr. nor Mrs. Richardson appeared. The police confirmed that the man I had wounded was indeed a terrorist wanted by the police for murder. He and the servants had all taken Mau-Mau oaths. I was first congratulated by the police, but then warned not to be too enthusiastic about shooting people. The prisoners were taken away in a police truck. The wounded man was taken to a hospital, where the bullet was extracted. He was later tried for murder, convicted and hanged.

At about 6:45 a.m. the following day, Mrs. Richardson was heard screaming for the servants. Dad walked over to explain that they had been housing a Mau-Mau gang, and all the gang members, including the servants had been arrested. Dad sarcastically added that the Richardsons would have to make their own cup of early morning tea. He further commented that it was unbelievable that the Richardsons had slept through the excitement, and he wondered what sleeping pills they used. Mr. Richardson mumbled that they had been awakened, but had not come out as they didn't want to get involved in a police raid. Dad replied that, if they had been awakened, they were probably short of Dutch courage despite the amount of booze they had consumed. He left them spluttering with indignation. The Richardsons left the area shortly after the incident.

***

I was earning a reputation for being fairly effective on anti-Mau-Mau operations - a good bum shot. The end of 1952 was in sight. I would turn twenty-two a few days before Christmas, and would be liable for conscription into the Kenya Regiment for a six months full time officer training course in Southern Rhodesia, where our attention would not be diverted by family affairs, romantic entanglements or business distractions. Contingents, each of 100 young white settlers were trained over periods of six months. Two contingents had already attended the course, and the training staff had become fully aware of the strengths and weaknesses of the Kenya European youth. The training they now delivered was first class. Each contingent was made up of eighteen and twenty-two year-olds, ensuring a significant percentage of more mature recruits.

2

The Draft

"I want to see you in my office at 9 o'clock," called out the boss of Dalgetys as he passed my desk upon his arrival one morning.

"Yes, Sir," I replied with apprehension rising.

I wanted to ask him why he had asked to see me, but he entered the elevator before I could gather my thoughts. He had never ordered me to see him in his office before. Had I offended a customer? Had I forgotten to do something? I went over the past few days trying to remember any occasion when I might have given cause for complaint or omitted to carry out some task. I found myself innocent, and this worried me still further as I would have to face the CEO without having thought up an excuse for any gaffe.

At the appointed hour I approached his secretary, a terse young woman, whose demeanor did nothing to allay my fears. Without a smile or greeting, she ushered me into the boss's office. Were my worst fears about to overtake me?

"Have you received your call-up papers yet?"

"Not yet, Sir," I replied with relief flooding through me. I hadn't committed a blooper. "I expect to get them any day now. Some pals of my age group have already received theirs."

"Well," he continued, "what I want to know is whether you'd prefer to do your six months military service, and then go to London for a year of further business training, or whether you'd like to go to London first, and then come back to do your training in the Kenya Regiment. We might even be able to avoid your having to do any military service by sending you to take over as branch manager in Dar es Salaam after you've been to London for a year. There's no call-up for the Kenya Emergency Service in Tanzania. Don't give me your answer now. Talk it over with your father and let me have your thoughts on the subject in a day or so."

"That won't be necessary, Sir," I replied, "I'd like to do my military service first, and then go to London."

"You're sure of this, are you? Because that's what we'd like you to do. I and the Company are keen to see you receive military training and are proud to release you for anti-Mau-Mau service. But you have to bear in mind that your service in the Kenya Regiment might be extended by the Emergency. No one knows how long this Mau-Mau thing is going to last, and you may be in the army for some time. I cannot guarantee what business training you may be asked to do after your military service, where you might be asked to do it, or for how long."

"I'm sure that I want to do my military training first, and I accept that the Company may have to change its plans for me if my service is extended."

"Well, if that's final, go ahead, and we'll see what we can do for you when you get back. Good luck, and mind you do come back. I mean, don't get yourself killed," he added. I was happy to learn that I was wanted.

I left Dalgetys believing it would be for a period of six months full-time military training. This was extended to eighteen months compulsory active service and then to over three years when I volunteered to stay on. Dalgetys promised to keep a place for me while I completed my military service. They had treated me well, and I was earning, after two years, double what had been promised if I completed four years. The Company agreed to make up any difference between my army pay and my Dalgety salary. I had enjoyed my service with the Company, and got on well with many of my colleagues. Dalgetys continued to contribute towards my retirement benefit fund all during my military service. I felt obliged to return to the company when I was finally released.

* * *

The Kenya Regiment was, in times of peace, a territorial unit. It was an organization that trained volunteers in basic army skills. I had been in the Officers' Training Corps (O.T.C.) when I was at high school, and had learned the basic elements of drill - how to walk forwards, turn left, turn right, and turn right round, stop, start, walk on the spot, and do all sorts of drill with a rifle, in addition to learning how to keep the weapons and ourselves clean, bright and slightly oiled. I had not been impressed with much of the O.T.C's. training, and hadn't volunteered for the Kenya Regiment, which made demands on weekend leisure-time and two of weeks full-time training each year.

Night patrols around our residential area had been exciting, and I looked forward to a period of anti-Mau-Mau Emergency Service after completion of military training. I had no great wish to spend a year in London, that vast, cold, gray city. Besides, I had fallen in love with the most delectable, curvaceous, blonde bombshell, Jennifer, and had hopes I might persuade her to enjoy ending our virginity in unison.

I looked forward to an exciting year fighting the Mau-Mau before I had to face a year in the bleak, alien London environment. It turned out I was to serve almost three and a half years, full-time military service, and the offer of commercial training in London and life with a beautiful, pulchritudinous blonde was scuttled forever. I received my draft papers, and was instructed to report to Kenya Regiment headquarters on 2nd January 1953 with a minimum of personal possessions.

I went to see Jennifer, and explained that I might die during the harsh training I was to undergo, and it might be a super idea if she was to enjoy a biological uproar with me. But she declined, and I left Kenya to face the mercies of a sergeant major with my virginity intact. I subsequently heard that Jennifer gave up her fight to defend her chastity shortly after I left for training in how to defend the British Empire.

3

Training in Southern Rhodesia (Zimbabwe)

The six month long course in Southern Rhodesia (now Zimbabwe) was based on the officers' training course held at Eton Hall near Chester in England, which trained young men called up for military service during the period when every able-bodied man in the UK had to do two years National Service.

We entered a life in which we were to be plagued by orders issued at the top of our instructors' roars. We learned to iron creases in our starched, green denim fatigues that were sharp enough to cause injury. We learned to polish brass and boots until they shone so brightly they would bring tears to the eyes. We learned to 'blanco' our webbing belts, straps, ammunition pouches and haversacks, and we learned a few bawdy army songs. We re-learned parade ground drill - how to walk forwards, turn right, turn left etc. We learned the importance of keeping our bowels open, all about 'cat sanitation' to be practiced when in the field, how to shout orders very loudly, how to clean our rifles, and then clean them again and again and again..........

We were told to wear clean underwear if we expected to get killed - so we would look decent when dead? Actually

I had heard that sudden death results in soiled underwear. If you were killed or wounded in action it was proof you had been idle in the face of the enemy or had failed to pay attention during training. You would not be regarded as a hero. A good soldier kills the enemy and does not waste the money that the tax payers have provided for military training by getting in the way of enemy fire.

We had to show we could climb a 16 ft rope, jump over a 16 foot 6 inch river, leap over a 3 foot 6 inch high gate, and run a mile in less than six minutes. We had to march six miles and then shoot at a target ten times, hitting the bulls-eye with each shot, all within an hour. Our squad marched the six miles in forty-two minutes, so we had plenty of time to get our breath back before settling down to shoot, without our aim being disturbed by panting from our exertions. We had to find our way through the bush using a map and compass. We had to be able to load a Bren magazine with twenty-five rounds in seven seconds, and fire twenty shots from a rifle in a minute.

The company of 100 recruits was split into four squads. I was in Number 4 Squad, which was comprised mainly of Nairobi-ites like me. We were considered the least likely to succeed, as it was assumed we had been pen pushers and desk pilots with no knowledge of bushcraft, hunting or shooting and other macho outdoor activities. It was true some of us fitted this description, but it was also true we had a fair share of above average intelligence. Our instructors were Sergeants Robertson and Bull. Perhaps they recognized there were physically unimpressive townies in the squad, and determined they would get a bit more than 100% from each of us.

Sgt. John Bull taught us a few tricks about spit and polish, so that our equipment shone brighter than that of the other squads, and he trained us to be the smartest on drill parade. Consequently, we were later to win the Drill Parade Cup.

A couple of weeks into our training the whole

Company was asked by the Education Officer to reply to the question as to whether drill, a smart turn-out and other bullshine was necessary. About 95% said it was all a waste of time, but some months into the course, the same question elicited a very different response, when we realized that we had been welded into a team by pride in our new-found smartness and capabilities.

Perhaps the common enemies, in the form of our Sergeant Instructors, also contributed to our initial attitude, but it is true to say, by the end of the course, we had become very loyal and quite attached to them. It never ceased to amaze me how Sgts. Bull and Robertson managed to train the members of 4 Squad into a well disciplined unit which was to win, not only the Drill Parade Cup, but also the Rifle Cup.

One of the men in 4 Squad had only recently arrived in Kenya when he was immediately conscripted into the Kenya Regiment. He had been a member of a London criminal gang, and when first issued with a rifle, said in a broad Cockney accent "Cor blimey, if me mates back in the East End could only see me now!"

When we went up onto the rifle range the first time we had to shoot at four foot square targets with a twelve inch diameter bull from 200 yards. The cockney thought the distance too great, so he aimed low. The slugs ricocheted off the ground before spinning into the target splattering it with small stones. This confused the men in the pits attending the targets, who first signaled that the target had been hit only to immediately signal a miss. Once the Cockney had been acquainted with the power of the rifle rounds, he still felt it necessary to pull the trigger violently, believing this would help the bullet to reach a target so far away. Eventually he was to become sufficiently proficient with both rifle and Bren light machine gun to pass the British Army tests.

Sgt. Robertson of the Black Watch Regiment had been a sniper for a record period of nine months during WWII. This highly stressful and dangerous job is usually limited to two month periods. Snipers are never taken prisoner. If caught, they are bayoneted in the guts or shot, and it is almost certain that sooner or later a sniper will meet his end. To have served as a sniper for such a long period, indicated an exceptional level of skill. Sgt. Robertson was a small man who could squeeze into hiding places which may have been overlooked.

Sgt. Robertson taught us how to shoot, and one tip he gave us was to stand me in good stead. We learned to adopt what he called a 'Zero Aiming Position.' To do this a right handed rifleman lay prone in an aiming position so the wrist of the left forearm was cradled against a sandbag or mound of earth in which an appropriately shaped indentation was made to accept the left wrist. The right elbow was then nudged into a comfortable indentation in the ground and the whole body shifted about so, after taking careful aim at the target, gently releasing one's grip, and then re-gripping the rifle, the aim was not disturbed. If the aim shifted, the body was squirmed into the ground and the necessary adjustments made so release of the grip on the rifle did not result in upsetting the aim. Practice in this method enabled us to adopt the 'Zero Aiming Position' quickly, and if correctly adopted, it was possible to fire shot after shot, operating the bolt between each shot with a smooth wrist action, without having to re-aim the rifle. It was only necessary to quickly check the aim had not been disturbed.

I was asked to carry out a rapid fire demonstration and I got off thirty-eight shots in thirty seconds hitting the 12 inch diameter bull with every shot from 200 yards. I'd have managed another two shots in the time had I not had a jam. The rounds were held in dispensable metal clips that each held five bullets. To charge the magazine, the clip was dropped into the breech, and using the thumb, the rounds were pressed down from the clip, which was flicked out by the thumb. The process was repeated with a second clip of five rounds, fully charging the magazine. These were not automatic or semi-automatic weapons but bolt-action Lee

Enfield .303 rifles. They were accurate, and practice in operating the bolt enabled a marksman to fire off a ten-round magazine accurately and reload quickly.

By using the Zero Aiming Position, I was able to carry out the rapid shooting demonstration. And it was this wrinkle that later enabled me to impress my pal, Don, to the extent that he invited me to accompany him on game hunting expeditions.

But I am running ahead and must get back to the time we were in Salisbury, Southern Rhodesia undergoing training.

4

The Lari Massacre

It was announced by our senior training officer that on 26th March 1953 at the Kikuyu village of Lari some twenty miles from Nairobi, a big gang had committed an appalling massacre. Over 100 Kikuyu villagers had been slaughtered by Mau-Mau terrorists. Pregnant women had their bellies slashed open, their fetuses ripped out and thrown to the ground before the eyes of the dying mothers. Victims were made to sit with heads bowed. Their heads were then severed slowly by *panga* (machete) wielding thugs. Children were among the dead, all of whom had been mutilated in unspeakable ways. The outrage was beyond all comprehension by most of the population of Kenya.

A police station in the little sleepy village of Naivasha was attacked, and firearms and ammunition were stolen. Included in the terrorist's haul were fully automatic sub-machine guns and a Bren Light Machine Gun (LMG). Later, these weapons were used by the terrorists in ambushes against military patrols in the Aberdare forest. The reports enraged us and we were eager to complete our training and get back to Kenya to fight the Mau-Mau.

5

We become a team

My life at boarding schools had prepared me for the ungracious living that was to be meted out by the permanent training corps, which consisted of experienced soldiers from British regiments. The Company Sergeant Major Joe (Grumble Guts) Cameron was a Scots Guardsman. We had sergeant instructors from the Grenadier Guards, the Black Watch and several famous English county regiments. I felt sorry for those of us who had never been away from home before, and those who were leaving the devoted attention of girlfriends.

***

One conscript in our contingent was a villain from Mombasa. Ken was a member of the Johnson Brothers' Gang. The gang consisted of two older brothers, who were always in trouble with the police, Ken, and occasionally other temporary members, when a proposed crime so required. The older brothers tried to keep Ken out of serious outlawry, but Ken had all the makings of a felon. He arrived at Kenya Regiment Headquarters with the rest of the contingent who were to fly to Salisbury (now Harare) in Southern Rhodesia (now Zimbabwe) the following day. We had our names and other particulars checked, were issued with uniforms and other kit, and underwent a medical examination. We listened to an officer who told us what training to expect, and had a short religious service conducted by the Regimental Padre. Then we were issued with straw palliasses and blankets and shown to a dormitory where we were to sleep the night. We were then free to lay out our palliasses on the floor, sort through our kit, and get to know each other.

Ken decided he didn't fit in with the rest of us, and bought himself a bottle of Scotch with which to console himself. Or was he really going to show us what a macho man he was? He became, by stages, friendly; tipsy; critical of the draft; morose; maudlin; drunk; boastful; belligerent; bellicose and insolent. He was put under arrest by the Regimental Police after a fight, during which he sustained superficial but painful injuries about his face. He spent the night in the guardhouse, and was only released when it was time to board the trucks which took us to the airport.

By the time we landed at Salisbury, he had sobered up, and had washed most of the blood from his face, neck and hands. But he appeared to have been run over by a tank, and was clearly sorry for himself. He staggered down the passenger steps, disheveled and sporting a bruised face and a swollen, discolored eye.

Company Sergeant Major, Joe 'Grumble Guts' Cameron, stood at the foot of the steps to meet us. He was obviously NOT impressed with the mishmash of un-soldierly rabble he was to have to train over the next six months. When he saw the dejected figure of Ken slouching painfully down the steps, Grumble Guts went ballistic. His worst fears were coming true. This contingent, epitomized by the dirty, disheveled, horrible little man who appeared before him, was undoubtedly the scrapings of the idle, villainous rascals from the bottom of the Kenya barrel.

In a broad Scottish accent, he shouted. He roared. He spluttered. He sobbed. None of us was able to make out a single word that issued from Grumble Guts. This was not entirely surprising - nobody ever can make out what N.C.Os. or Warrant Officers in the British Army shout. But we understood very well the sight of Ken did not please Grumble Guts, and we were all likely to suffer as a consequence. Ken was still too dopey and hungover to fully appreciate his circumstances. He just wished the rather frightening CSM would speak, in English, more quietly.

***

Ken's two older brothers were in hospital in Mombasa in Kenya. They had been arrested, charged and convicted of some crime for which they were to be incarcerated in one of Her Majesty's prisons for several years. The prison was Fort Jesus, which had been built by the Portuguese in the 16th Century. It is on Mombasa Island and stands on a rocky part of the shore, guarding the entry to Mombasa's Old Port. The crenellated walls rise sheer from the rocks to a height of some fifty feet. They are windowless and have no niches to enable, even the most skilled rock climber, to find foot or handholds. Inside the prison, the walls rise about fifteen feet above the rough courtyard off which are the prisoners' cells, administration offices, warders' quarters and stores.

It was mandatory for every prisoner to plait twenty feet per day of coconut palm frond leaves into two inch wide strips. These were used in the weaving of charpoys (cots with wooden legs and frames) for junior government employees wherever they were serving in Kenya. Failure to complete twenty feet of braided strip by a prisoner resulted in the denial of food. Naturally, prisoners soon became skilled in the task, and the two Johnson brothers, who had spent several stretches in prison previously, were well able to complete the required footage - and more.

They decided to escape. I learned of their escapade from newspaper reports and from Ken who befriended me when I berated him on the occasion when he drank himself

The Great Escape. Brother #2 prepares for a soft landing on brother #1.

silly on the night we reported to Kenya Regiment Headquarters. Everyone else had ignored him. To my regret, Ken seemed to regard me as his trusted mentor. Ken received frequent letters from his mother who kept him up-to-date with news of the regressive vicissitudes of his wayward brothers.

Using, perhaps, the only skill they had, the two brothers plaited extra lengths of strip each day. They managed to hide the extra lengths, which they spliced onto the other extra lengths they made daily. Soon they had a long 'escape rope'. They had assessed the length they needed to tie round one of the crenellations at the top of the wall to hang down the outer side of the wall to the rocks fifty feet below.

They chose night time to lessen the chance of their being seen by a prison warder. How they managed to unlock their cell door is not known. They crept through the courtyard, keeping to the darkest shadows, and climbed a staircase leading to a gallery eight feet below the top of the wall. There they tied the rope securely to one of the crenellations, a job which took somewhat more rope than they had allowed for. No matter. There was plenty of rope. Brother #1 climbed up, grabbed the rope firmly and began to lower himself hand over hand, down the outside of the wall.

Brother #2 was supposed to wait until brother #1 signaled, by shaking the rope, that he had successfully completed his fifty foot descent. But a guard appeared, and started up the staircase to the gallery, so brother #2 also clambered over the crenellations, and began his descent. Both brothers now realised the rope was not actually designed to take the weight of two fully grown men, and there was more than a slight chance of the palm leaves slipping and the rope parting.

Neither brother knew anything about rappelling, nor the advantage of 'walking backwards' down, so the rope is held away from the wall. The darkness was now a disadvantage. They couldn't see the rope below them, and were unable to wrap the rope around their flailing legs to take some of their weight from their tiring hands and arms. They barked their knuckles and banged their knees on the wall. Ominous sounds came from the rope. Was it about to part? They hurried on down.

Suddenly brother #1 came to the end of the rope. He had no idea how much further down were the rocks. He let go. There was a sickening sound as he hit the rocks twenty feet below and an ankle fractured. He lay there in agony. He was unable to move or let his brother know their assessment of the length of the rope was twenty feet short.

Brother #2 came to the end of the rope. He also let go. He had a slightly softer landing as he fell on his brother. There was a nauseating sound of ribs cracking and another ankle being wrenched.

The sounds of falling brothers alerted the warder, and the Johnson brothers were recaptured. They recovered from their breakages in a hospital, and were re-incarcerated, with additional time for attempting to escape. The tale gives some idea as to how inept the Johnsons were. On our arrival at Salisbury Airport, Ken had gained black marks from Grumble Guts, and had brought down disapproval on whole contingent.

***

Ken was a poor physical specimen, and had no chance of passing the minimum standard tests required by the British Army. The first of these was to climb up a sloping rope, transfer to a horizontal rope sixteen feet above ground, swing hand over hand across an eighteen foot long rope, and then descend down another sloping rope to the ground. Ken struggled up the first sloping rope, but fell while attempting to transfer to the horizontal rope. Fortunately, he landed on soft ground, not ankle shattering rock as had his brothers. Ken was shaken, but not stirred to attempt the other tests. He was advised to report sick, and so missed them.

When we carried out forced marches, Ken hung onto my belt to be towed along. This enabled him to keep up with us and complete the marches, but not without vomiting down the backs of my fatigues. I suffered in silence for the good of the squad. It was amazing how quickly a team spirit had been instilled into all members of our squad.

I got back at Ken to some extent when he had a fight with a much smaller man, Roy. What the fight was about, I never found out, but it was at a time when Ken was beginning to realise he had some faults, and he had become even more boastful to compensate. He had possibly bragged to Roy about some imagined feat, and Roy was likely to have retorted tersely to imply that Ken was a liar, and that he should take a hike. Whatever the reasons, a fight ensued. Ken insisted on a wrestling match since Roy had a reputation as an able boxer. Roy had conceded to Ken's wish, which put him at a disadvantage as Ken was nearly twice Roy's weight.

The struggle ended in a draw with neither gladiator able to gain a winning hold. I arrived on the scene about this time, and saw two panting contestants at an impasse. What prompted me to do so, I don't know. I ordered them to separate. Once they had regained their feet, I broke into a tirade in which I castigated both of them, pointing out we were supposed to be a team, and internal dissension did not augur well for our future inter-squad competitions. I then asked a few questions, and learned that wrestling had been Ken's choice. This led me to turn on him with all guns blazing.

"What a pathetic milksop you are. You can't beat a man half your weight, even when you choose to wrestle. Roy would have given you the thrashing of your life had you agreed to box. We, all of us, are sick and tired of your lies, bragging, worthless efforts and feeble behavior. You are a wretched coward. Why don't you take on somebody our own size and weight? I would dearly love to give you the hammering you deserve. And for goodness sake, in future, be sick BEFORE we go on a forced march. Or, better still, don't eat before a march. Or better yet, don't eat at all. Starve yourself to death. Just go away and die."

I turned on my heel and strode away. Perhaps Ken was ashamed, of his not being able to pass the British Army Tests, of having to be towed on forced marches and vomiting from the effort, of being unable to overcome Roy, and of having all his boasting proved hollow.

Ken changed. He was much quieter, and often could be seen in deep thought. He no longer spent every night in the bar. He spent more time cleaning his brass buttons and badges, polishing his boots, blanco-ing his webbing, ironing his fatigues, and cleaning his rifle. He became so quiet we almost forgot him, and when we did notice his presence, we raised our eyes heavenwards and sighed with relief at the changes. By degrees, Ken became fitter, and by the time our training period was over, Ken had become a reasonable team member.

On our return to Kenya after our six month training course, we were all sent off to different units. I lost track of Ken, but understand he served in the Kenya Regiment Stores, and gained the rank of corporal under the Quartermaster Sergeant. A year after we had returned from training in Southern Rhodesia, by which time I had been promoted to Captain, I was in Nairobi on a forty-eight hour furlough when I bumped into Ken. He was to be discharged from military service that day. I was impressed by his corporal's stripes and commended him.

"Now," I said, "don't be a damned fool and get into trouble with the law. Get a decent job and stick at it. Keep away from your stupid brothers. Learn a trade. Work hard. Be reliable."

"Yes, Captain Gill," he replied. "My brothers are still in prison, and I've learned my lesson."

"You used to call me Len," I commented. "What's all this Captain Gill?"

"As I said, I've learned my lesson." Ken smiled and we parted.

Later that day, immediately after his discharge, Ken stole a small car. He had driven it twenty miles out of town before it ran out of gas. Leaving the car by the side of the road, he caught a lift to the next town taking a two gallon can from the trunk. After filling the can, he caught a lift back to the stolen car, and began to pour the gas into the tank. Five African constables under command of an African sergeant sprang from nearby bushes and arrested the astonished Ken. He faced trial, conviction and a prison sentence.

***

Number 4 Squad became so proficient at shooting that we won competitions. The hunters in the other squads claimed we were successful only because we were shooting on a rifle range. Under active service conditions against moving targets, we would be lost. We would not be able to get down into a prone position, but would have to shoot from a standing position, and would have to get off a shot very quickly. My bird shooting experience with an air rifle, enabled me to hit moving targets from a standing position with a high level of success.

I was to do much practice shooting with rifles, Brens and Sten sub-machine guns after being posted to the King's African Rifles (KAR) when we returned to Kenya after our six months training. Much of this practice shooting was done in jungle ranges at pop-up and swinging targets. I lived with my firearm, taking it with me wherever I went. Its weight and shape became ingrained; it became part of me, and I could bring it into action quickly, smoothly and accurately.

After completing eight weeks 'Basic Training', one man from each squad was promoted to Lance Corporal. This was a temporary rank, carried no extra wage, and was designed to test leadership skills. I was the first in 4 Squad to gain this rank, which meant that I now had to give orders, check everyone was on parade and weapons were clean, bright and slightly oiled. We held the rank for a couple of weeks, and then relinquished it so some other soldier could have the opportunity to be tested.

**

We thought we got the better of Company Sergeant Major Joe (Grumble Guts) Cameron one day when all four squads were on the parade-ground practicing slow-marching. This requires the toe to be pointed to the ground as each step is taken. We had been issued with steel toe-capped boots, and however much one strained to point one's toe, the bulging toe cap appeared to stick up. Grumble Guts watched our performance, and his temper and color rose to danger point. Finally, screaming like a banshee, he had all four squads fall into two ranks, and he slow-marched us across the parade-ground calling out 'toe' with each step to remind us to point our toes. Well, that is what he ordered us to do, but 100 voices, all trained to shout out orders at maximum volume, yelled "JOE, JOE, JOE".

Grumble Guts took off his cap and threw it and his pace-stick to the ground. He jumped on his cap, stamped and screamed, while we continued to slow march shouting "JOE, JOE, JOE" until we reached the far side of the parade-ground. Grumble Guts retrieved his crushed cap and pace-stick, and stormed off in high dudgeon. Our sergeant instructors formed us into our four squads again, and we continued with our drill practice with just a few outbreaks of sniggering. I suspect it was all put on by Grumble Guts and our instructors, and it was probably our sergeant instructors who first started yelling "JOE, JOE, JOE".

Grumble Guts tried to ensure every recruit came before the Company Commander for some minor offense. His choice of punishment was almost always the same. One had to clean a steel baking tray from the kitchen. The trays

We became skilled baking tray cleaners.

were 24" x 18" x 4" deep, and were always covered in a thick layer of burnt-on grease and fat, which was very difficult to remove.

We became quite skilled at cleaning them. The smallest man in the squad sat in the tray as a 'weight', and was pushed around on the sandy soil outside the back of the barrack rooms. The weight, who had the makings of a contortionist, then varied his position by crouching down on one side and then the other of the tray to be pushed/pulled around. In no time the bottom and all sides were abraded clean, and attention was turned to the inside, which was never too difficult to clean with sand and soap. In this manner the trays were cleaned in minutes rather than hours. Perhaps it was Grumble Guts intention to test our ability to work as a team to find a method to present a tray that looked almost new and was bound to pass inspection.

Grumble Guts caught me being 'idle on parade', an offense which covered everything from being slovenly to just being there. He ordered me to report to the Company Commander's Office the following morning. I noticed he failed to make a note of my name. I also noticed he caught about six other men for the same offense. So, I failed to appear at the Company office, and thus evaded punishment and preserved an unblemished record.

***

During the last couple of weeks of our training we marched, at night, thirty-nine miles to Inkomo, an established army training area. In those days the Rhodesian roads were made up of two 18 inch wide tarmac strips. The road on either side and between these strips was 'metalled'. That is to say, these areas were surfaced with two-inch hard stones, embedded in the clay. When vehicles approached each other, they were both expected to slow and leave the tarmac strips and drive along the metalled parts on each side and center of the road.

We wore hob-nailed boots with steel tipped heels, and neither these nor the road, had any give in them. Furthermore, the tarmac was broken away at the edges in many places, the metalled surfaces were potholed. Many of the stones stood proud, making for a very uneven surface. Marching in the dark, it was impossible to avoid these hazards. This resulted in damage to our feet.

One soldier was withdrawn from the march when each step produced a sickening squelch caused by blood from burst blisters. When we reached our destination after thirteen hours, we were ordered to remove our boots for a foot inspection. Many of us were unable to put our boots on again, owing to massive swelling of our painful, weary feet. They recovered during the night, and we were able to carry out maneuvers the next day.

These consisted of war games entailing creeping around with colored armbands to indicate which side you were on, and pretending to shoot 'the enemy'. This was the sort of game Mike Duggins and I had played when we were a seven years old. I was pretty expert and saw, in many cases, the best approach towards the 'enemy' was through areas designated as 'minefields' or 'out-of-bounds' by our instructors.

Such an area was a firing range used by the Rhodesian Air Force. I saw that this would make a good approach to a place from which I could observe the 'enemy', but was terrified when a Spitfire fighter of the Rhodesian Air Force came over very fast at ground level, firing rockets into a 12 ft. high built-up bank, rather like a large golf bunker. I took cover behind another bunker and then ran, as fast as my panic-stricken legs would carry me, to the next bank between each rocket firing run. I made it across the range with the firm decision not to return that way.

From my observation place, which I would never have reached by any other route, I watched the 'enemy' and saw to my amazement they were using a high watchtower as an observation post from which they could cover a wide angle. I had thought they would not use such an obvious target as a vantage point. Making an undetected approach to the watchtower, through 'legitimate' areas, was difficult. I worked out an approach along which I thought I might make an unseen arrival at the foot of the tower, and radioed my intentions, without divulging my location or how I'd got there. I anticipated my side now knew they would have to lie low until the outcome of my final approach to the foot of the watchtower was known.

My stalk up to the foot of the tower was successful, despite my having to cross two areas with very sparse cover. When I reached the tower, I was surprised to be met by three of my own side, who had made a successful approach from a different direction. We quietly climbed the stairs leading to the room at the top of the tower. On reaching the top landing, I gently pushed the door open, and we peered in to find that all three 'enemy' observers were asleep. From my ammo pouch I took a thunderflash, a powerful firecracker that is used to simulate a hand grenade in war games.

A thunderflash is set off by striking it on a board like a safety match. One has a few seconds between striking and the explosion. It is quite a dangerous toy that can blow off a finger. I lobbed the thunderflash into the room, and was horrified to see it roll against one of the 'enemy'. It exploded, blowing off his webbing ammo pouch, which saved him from harm. All three were deemed to have been killed. We occupied the watchtower, and directed our side in a successful battle against the 'enemy'. They had failed to set up any more observation posts in addition to the one in the watchtower.

The 'enemy' was most incensed by the dangerous act that I had committed in throwing a thunderflash into the room. But they dropped this accusation when we mentioned that their observers had all been asleep. When asked about my approach to the watchtower, I played mute, and when interrogation became more insistent, the chief referee cut it short by saying, whatever my method, it was acceptable in view of the fact that all's fair in love and war.

***

At the end of the six month course, we returned to Kenya and were granted two weeks leave. In a romantic haze, I took the curvaceous blonde bombshell, Jennifer, down to the coast, and her mother came too.

Jennifer's mum's presence didn't prevent me succeeding in my long held hope of gaining admittance to Jennifer's up-until-now 'never' regions. But my success was hollow. The wanton wench admitted she had enjoyed partying in the company of draft-dodgers with whom she had ended her virginity.

I cursed the drones who idled their time in Nairobi, entertaining the girls we had left behind. Many of them wore holstered guns saying they had to travel to dangerous areas in the course of their employment. They flaunted their guns to impress. Many had avoided the draft on flimsy pretexts: Jobs vital to the economy; supporting aged relatives; incurable ailments and disabilities; suddenly acquired conscientious or religious objections and attendance at educational or specialist training courses. We judged them to be young, healthy but cowardly.

6

4th (Uganda) Battalion of the Kings African Rifles

After my holiday, I was promoted to sergeant, and posted to the 4th (Uganda) Battalion of the King's African Rifles as a platoon commander. A platoon commander is usually a Second Lieutenant, another temporary rank. That is to say that both L/Cpls. and 2nd Lts. are on probation. A sergeant, with officer potential, might serve as a platoon commander, pending being commissioned. I joined No. 1 Platoon of 'A' Company of the 4th KAR in July 1953. Unfortunately, within a day or two of my arrival, I was struck down by an acute attack of malaria and was sent to hospital.

The platoon was temporarily commanded by Sergeant, Bruce Brown, who seemed to me unsuitable for the job. He appeared irresolute and nervous. Bruce had served in the British Army vehicle maintenance corps, and had never been in action. He was not a Kenya lad, had only recently arrived from England, had almost immediately been conscripted into the Kenya Regiment, and was promptly seconded to the 4th KAR. He had no knowledge of Swahili. Being the only European in command of an isolated platoon of Africans made him feel alone among strangers. He failed to show leadership when danger threatened.

The platoon was camped in an empty warehouse some four miles from Company HQ. A barbed wire fence had been erected around the building, and within the fence, trenches had been dug. Before dawn one morning, a large gang of Mau-Mau passed by the camp. The guard awakened the men and the platoon manned the trenches. Bruce claimed every automatic firearm: Three Brens and three Patchetts had jammed. Actually, he had refused to give the order to open fire. The outcome was the platoon was visited by the Adjutant and Medical Officer, who determined Bruce had suffered a mental breakdown. He was returned to England.

I recovered quickly under medical treatment, and returned to my platoon. I was now in the deep end as platoon commander over thirty African soldiers. The platoon's morale was low, and I knew I'd have to prove myself.

Initially, I had some apprehensions with regard to the loyalty of my Ugandan soldiers toward me, a European settler. I had no idea how my men would behave in action. Would they take the opportunity to kill me? There was one Kenya Regiment soldier serving with African troops who had been killed in action in suspicious circumstances. But I had heard he was one of those who liked to 'kick ass'. Maybe one of his men had become incensed with his bullying ways. What could my soldiers expect from me? Would I show leadership under all conditions? How would I behave when we came under fire? Would I treat my men fairly? Would I understand their problems? As Ugandans, they were serving in a foreign country, Kenya. Did I understand how they felt about this? What did I know about soldiering? Was I just another arrogant, uncaring, imperious, hateful European?

The mental breakdown of the Sgt. Bruce Brown had raised doubts among the African soldiers as to the qualities of Kenya Regiment men. The fluency of my Swahili improved as the weeks went by. As the only European in a platoon of African troops, I spoke nothing but Swahili, except when I reported to our company commander by radio.

※ ※ ※

I had no clear orders as to what patrolling was to be done. We were not allowed to enter the forest as the size of the Mau-Mau gang close to our camp was believed to be in the order of 800 - too many for a platoon of thirty to engage. I was to deny passage through the 'One Mile Area' to the enemy. This was the cleared farmland one mile from the forest edge marked by a line of white posts. Anybody within the 'One Mile Area' or in the forest was to be shot on sight.

Bracken fern had grown up in the 'One Mile Area', and I took a patrol into the bracken to find that it was up to seven feet high and almost impenetrable. I struggled through the matted bracken, making a path for the rest of the patrol, northwards and parallel to the forest edge. I determined that there were no recent trails through the bracken from the forest to the area occupied by Kikuyu peasant farmers. They might be intimidated into supplying food and clothing to the terrorists.

There was an old logging road from the farming area across the 'One Mile Area' into the forest. Examination of the road showed this also to be devoid of human tracks. I was at a loss as to what action I could take against the Mau-Mau. They seemed not to be passing through my area, although intelligence reports indicated gang activity in the forest.

To the south, the road to the platoon's base continued through the 'One Mile Area' to the forest. It went through the forest, over the Aberdare mountain range to European-owned farms on the western slopes. It was along this track, called the Bamboo Road, which the big gang had recently made its way past our platoon camp into the forest. A few yards further south of this road a gorge ran parallel to the road. To the south of the gorge was an area patrolled by another KAR battalion.

Against orders, I took my patrol along the Bamboo Road, but it was clear that it was not in regular use by the terrorists. We approached the rim of a gorge to the south of the road, and I peered into it with my binoculars. I saw a narrow trail, running beside the river, which appeared to have been used. I always carried binoculars on patrol. My comrades-in-arms thought me mad as the distance one could see in the forest or in bracken or bush, was very limited. But, on several occasions, I was able to avoid discovery or followed tracks by using binoculars with which I could make out telltale signs, without exposing my patrol's position.

Following tracks made by bare feet is not always easy, and the chasm was deep. Even using binoculars, I was not certain the trail was being used by the Mau-Mau. I decided to take a closer look later, but was reluctant to take a patrol down into the chasm, as it appeared it would be a dangerous climb over slippery rocks and through bushes clinging to the cliff. We might be mistaken for terrorists by the neighboring unit operating to the south of the canyon. I felt I could not risk the lives of my African troops.

Later that day, feeling vulnerable, I made a lone reconnaissance. I found an easy climb down into the gorge, used by game animals. I reached the trail at the bottom of the canyon more easily than I had anticipated. With a pounding heart, I made an inspection of the trail, confirmed it was in regular use by the enemy, who faced death if seen in the proscribed area. I started a regular evening routine. Without someone to watch my back, I felt undefended when I set out daily at about 5.00 p.m. to creep through thick cover to a convenient ledge just below the rim of the canyon. Using a .303 rifle fitted with a 'scope', I lay on the ledge and awaited the appearance of terrorists.

For nearly four weeks, almost every day, usually alone, terrorists appeared on the track at the foot of the gorge. It was easy to pick them off, usually with a single shot, from about 150 yards as they made their way slowly along the twisting path. Where they were going and why they were nearly always alone, I didn't know. I suspected they were taking messages to terrorists elsewhere, or on food foraging excursions. They were armed with *pangas*, and either a short spear or a bow with poisoned arrows.

Before darkness fell each evening I returned to camp, and taking a couple of soldiers, climbed down to drag the bodies of the dead terrorists away from the river into a spur gorge. We collected their weapons and any documents they had on them. We shredded their clothing to deny its use by other terrorists. After a couple of days the corpses began to decompose. The stench funneled up the spur gorge, and went unnoticed by the terrorists, who continued to use the track almost every evening. Later the corpses were washed down the river during a big flood. They may have fed crocs a few miles downstream.

I gained the respect of my men because I was prepared to make my way alone to take up the position from which I covered the gorge. Proof of my successes was evident when I took men down into the gorge to drag the bodies away from the river.

My sniping ended when I failed to kill one terrorist of a group of three as they came along the track one evening. Two fell to my rifle, but the third turned and disappeared behind boulders. I supposed he reported to his gang, and they realized what had been happening to their comrades over the past weeks.

I felt I had, to some extent, avenged the death of many innocent victims of vile Mau-Mau terrorism in the Lari massacre.

7

KAR rations and equipment

The 4th KAR had been brought down from Uganda, ill equipped for jungle warfare. They wore standard army hob-nailed leather boots, so silent patrolling was virtually impossible. No sleeping bags were issued, and nights out in the forest, where frost was common, took a toll on health when men developed rasping coughs.

Rations were based on *posho* (ground maize) and canned corned beef, supplemented with stinging nettles to make soup. Occasionally we enjoyed the meat of a bush buck which I shot. A decision had to be made: Shoot for the pot to nourish us, but perhaps alert the terrorists.

We carried Mark IV Lee Enfield .303 rifles. A Patchett sub-machine-gun was issued to each section radio operator. The Patchetts were improved WWII Sten sub-machine-guns firing 9 mm pistol bullets from a magazine that held thirty-four rounds. Designed for close-range and house-clearing roles, they were not accurate and lacked power. On more than one occasion, terrorists survived being hit by a burst. The ammunition was old and I wondered with what ammunition the British forces were issued. The 9mm round has a fairly good reputation, but I found the ammunition, manufactured ten years earlier, almost useless.

Later, when the 3rd KAR returned from active service in Malaya, the 4th KAR went back to Uganda, and our rations and equipment improved. The new rations were based on *mchele* (rice) instead of *posho*. Canvas, rubber-soled jungle boots were issued together with water-proofed light but warm sleeping bags. Mark V short-barrelled .303 rifles replaced the longer Mark IV models. The short barreled rifles were easier to swing into action in thick undergrowth. More Patchetts were issued, but still with the old, ineffectual ammunition left over from WWII.

***

As my platoon and I got to know each other better, I felt it imperative we carry out aggressive patrols against the enemy. Intelligence indicated there was still a large gang in the forest adjacent to our platoon base, and we were still under orders not to patrol into the forest. I spoke to my African Sergeant, Gideon, and asked if he thought any of the men might volunteer to accompany me into the forest on a reconnaissance. He was enthusiastic about the idea.

I had been successful in sniping, but my men had seen no action. Sgt. Gideon asked how many men I wanted to go with me, and I suggested one section of ten men, as I wanted to move quietly without verbal orders. I suggested a few hand signals, realizing that the undergrowth would slow communications throughout a large patrol. A small patrol, in which we would all be within visual range most of the time, seemed to offer better chances of success.

I armed myself with a child's toy in the form of a 'clicker', with which to attract my troops' attention. It was one of those metal devices that, held between thumb and forefinger and squeezed, make a metallic click which is repeated when the pressure is released. Operated quickly, the distinctive double 'click click' carried well in the forest. Though the enemy may have heard it, they never seemed to realise it was a man-made sound.

The whole platoon volunteered to come with me, so I picked the ten men in No.1 Section, promising the others they would have their chance later. We discussed patrolling methods and formations, and trained for two days, rested for one day, and left base at 4 a.m. on the fourth day, to enter the forest in darkness. I left Sgt. Gideon in command of our base.

We took a small VHF radio/transmitter with us so we could maintain contact with Sgt. Gideon. A couple of hundred yards into the forest we halted, and sat in the wet undergrowth to await daylight. I allowed no smoking or talking, not even whispering, which so often develops into talking.

The only sound was of the rain dripping from the trees. Cold water dribbled down inside my clothes. I wanted to continue our advance before I became chilled. Did I really want to move on - into danger? I had seen men die - and wounded men writhing in pain. Anyone who says they are not frightened by death is either a liar or mad. It was dying more than death itself that I feared.

I was more scared of appearing cowardly. As a platoon commander, I couldn't show fear. I sat huddled, sharing conditions and feelings with my African comrades: The discomfort, the creeping coldness, the eerie silence, the fear of an engagement with an unknown number of terrorists, and the worry as to how well we would control our fear. I felt close to my men. I wondered how they were feeling and if they were having similar thoughts.

The men recruited for the KAR came from warrior tribes. They were stoical beyond belief. I had a vision of myself lying wounded in wet, cold grass. Would I be able to emulate a warrior's disregard for the torment of, say, a gut wound? I was a lone European among courageous African tribesmen. Their attitude to anyone who screams, moans or sobs when in pain, might lead them to feel the wounded one is not worthy of life. Not worthy of saving. I would rather be killed than to suffer without the dignity I knew they would show. My parents wanted me to live. Would they have understood my dread of behaving despicably, in the eyes of my African comrades.

Were my troops plagued with such thoughts, or did they shrug off fear and simply face whatever came, with steadfast patience in the knowledge that they had no control over fate. I pushed these thoughts from my mind and glanced about me to see, in the gathering light, my men sitting quietly. Some grinned at me, and the closeness I had sensed earlier increased. I smiled back, and rose to my feet, ready to accept whatever came my way.

As the sun rose, we smelled smoke from a wood fire, and with utmost caution advanced toward it. We had covered barely 400 yards when I spotted a camp about seventy yards ahead. We crouched down, and I surveyed the scene with my binoculars, looking for a sentry. It seemed the terrorists had not been attacked in their camp in the forest before, and had become over confident. No sentries had been posted.

They had lit fires to prepare a meal. I signaled to each of my men, ensured they had all seen the enemy, and made hand-signal instructions as to where each man was to position himself. I then gave the signal to quietly fix bayonets. We rose to our feet and began to creep toward the enemy. They were chatting quite loudly, and were gathered around fires where meat was being roasted.

Using the undergrowth as cover, we got within about 40 yards of the main body of the gang. We could now see there were about forty terrorists. I wished I'd brought a larger patrol. Some were making their way out of camp to answer calls of nature. Sooner or later we would certainly be seen, and lose the advantage of surprise. Furthermore, we were very close if a counter attack was mounted. On my signal, my men took up positions from where they had a clear view of the enemy.

I opened fire. A volley from my men poured into

the surprised gang, most of who fled into the forest. After further volleys, I led a charge through the enemy camp, noting several bodies lying around the area of the fires. After a seventy yard charge, I recalled my men back to the enemy camp, which we searched for arms, ammunition, food and hidden terrorists. I posted three sentries to guard three prisoners, and cursed myself for the small number of men in my patrol.

With the rest of the patrol, I made an effort to follow the tracks of the fleeing gang, but they had split up, and following one man was likely to be time consuming and dangerous for our small team. We returned to the three men guarding the prisoners. The bodies of the dead were dragged to a collection point and searched. We gathered documents, removed clothing, burned it and the food. I contacted our platoon base by radio and reported our success.

We had killed six terrorists and captured three. I was sure we had wounded others. Carrying captured weapons, we withdrew to our platoon base. It was apparent a small patrol had one major disadvantage. To follow fleeing enemy when some of the patrol had to guard prisoners was risky.

The terrorist prisoners were interrogated before being handed over to the Kikuyu Home Guard for further questioning. They were all shot later that day 'while trying to escape.' This was to be the pattern throughout the Emergency. I stopped handing prisoners over to the Kikuyu Guard, who should have been the best interrogators since they were familiar with the locale, and the people who normally lived there. Instead, I handed prisoners over to the police, who were disciplined, and were trained to deal fairly.

Feuds dealt with by Kikuyu Guards

The Kikuyu have a long history of inter-family *fatina* (feuds), and many captured Mau-Mau terrorists, handed over to the Kikuyu Guard, all too frequently came to an untimely end when a *fatina* was settled by members of the KG. This summary justice was, perhaps, a sort of *quid pro quo* against the continuing problem of the Mau-Mau committing ghastly outrages in their efforts to terrorize potential recruits into joining their movement.

The KG was made up of loyal Kikuyu, and they, together with those they protected, were to suffer at the hands of the Mau-Mau to a greater extent than any other community. When presented with an excuse to kill terrorists, the KG also sought to settle *fatinas*. They adopted the attitudes that, since prisoners who had been captured in the forest were subject to being hanged after a hearing in a court of law, why bother with the court case? So they claimed *fatina* enemies to have been captured in proscribed areas and terminated the life of the prisoner. If I reported cases of murder by the KG, I was told I would provoke misunderstandings and mistrust among the very people whose loyalty we were trying to gain. Therefore my reports were ignored.

Later we were to carry out training of the Kikuyu Guards, who were issued with single-barreled, single-shot 12 gauge shotguns and SG (buckshot) cartridges. These discharged nine balls each of about quarter inch diameter. They were lethal at short range, and inflicted disabling wounds at ranges up to 200 feet. Once the KG was given training in shooting, the laying of ambushes and other skills, they made a significant contribution in crushing the Mau-Mau terrorists.

8

Interference by politicians

Left-wing politicians in Britain and Kenya were claiming there were atrocities being committed by members of the anti-Mau-Mau security forces. They alleged, given time, they could bring about a political resolution to the Mau-Mau problem. They seemed indifferent to the fact the terrorists were wreaking murder and mayhem among their own people.

The politicians feigned rage when they learned patrol commanders recorded kills and captures. During WWII, allied fighter pilots stuck decals on their aircraft to denote the number of enemy aircraft they had destroyed. Likewise, patrol commanders in Kenya kept records of successes on chalkboards in their platoon headquarters. We were ordered to stop the practice as it was deemed to jeopardize possible political mediation. In court cases, some captured terrorists were acquitted on legal technicalities, and were set free when defense attorneys demanded evidence that simple soldiers had failed to record in writing.

The result of the politicians' complaints and the acquittals of terrorists was that some of the Security Forces stopped keeping records, and some kills were not reported. If reports were made, a considerable number of man-hours were employed in paperwork to satisfy the queries raised by the politicians, who were perceived by members of the Security Forces to be treacherous traitors. Ongoing murder and mutilation by the terrorists was apparently to be to be overlooked while the politicians were given time to show off their political negotiating skills.

The Security Forces were well-disciplined, but as in all violent confrontations there are a few who will take the opportunity to satisfy their psychotic urge to kill. A serious result of the politicians' complaints was that crimes by members of the Security Forces were hidden in the mass of unreported kills.

For example, our Company Commander, Maj. John Bramston, and his second-in-command, Capt. Mike Harris, were both pathological killers, and their behavior reinforced the Kikuyu Guards' inclination to end family feuds by terminating the lives of those they could claim as Mau-Mau.

My platoon captured a terrorist in the forest, and we brought him to our camp for questioning. I reported the capture to Company HQ by radio, and Bramston raced round to my camp to help in extracting intelligence about the captured terrorist's gang. He threw the man into a trench, snatched my firearm from me, and aimed it at the terrified prisoner. I started forward to try to prevent Bramston from shooting the wretch, but was too late. Bramston fired, and I was relieved to see the bullet strike the wall of the trench an inch above the man's head. Bramston claimed his idea was to soften-up the prisoner so he would talk. But I had already extracted all the information the prisoner was able to give.

I regarded Bramston's visit to my platoon to be an opportunity to show me how to treat prisoners. Members of the Kikuyu Guard, including the headman from the nearby Kikuyu Guard Post, had seen Bramston's act, and asked if they could take the prisoner for further interrogation. Bramston had noted my distaste for his behavior. He agreed to their request. We watched as they escorted the man toward their camp. No sooner had they disappeared from view behind a hut than there was a shot.

"What happened?" I yelled.

"The prisoner was shot dead - while trying to escape," was the shouted reply.

Bramston had known what was likely to happen to the prisoner. He grinned and left the scene. No report was made of the prisoner's demise.

***

General Headquarters in Nairobi finally gave orders that we were to carry out a sortie into the forest. In full company strength under Bramston's command, we left Company HQ at 2 a.m., and marched under cover of darkness in heavy rain into the forest. This was to ensure that we were not seen by the enemy. Once in the forest, the rain and darkness made further progress impossible, so we halted.

To my amazement, on Bramston's orders, fires were lit, an astounding accomplishment in heavy rain. Fifteen ex-Mau-Mau terrorists, borrowed from the Police, had been pressed into service with our company. They were carrying the dismantled components of a 3" mortar, and a quantity of 3" mortar bombs strapped in packs of four. These men, using their *pangas*, dug down through arms length of forest debris to bamboo roots, which were dry. Sheltering them with their bodies, the ex-Mau-Mau twisted the roots to form dry tinder. Once this was lit, it was not difficult to get fires burning. For some reason which escaped me, it seemed we were no longer interested in keeping our whereabouts secret. Surely the smoke from our fires would attract the attention of any nearby Mau-Mau.

As the sun rose, we set off in single file up a slippery game track. It was virtually impossible to control eighty-five men strung out over some 350 feet along a twisting jungle trail. A herd of elephant, startled by our approach, crashed across our path. Surely the enemy now knew where we were, and the direction of our advance. The situation worsened when we were obliged to climb over the bamboo knocked down by the fleeing elephants. As we made our way obliquely up the side of a valley along a well defined game trail, we were ambushed from our right. A section of the enemy was armed with weapons acquired when they raided the police station at Naivasha.

They allowed the leading platoon to pass through the ambush and then opened up on my platoon from thick bush a few yards off the track. A section of *panga*-armed terrorists then charged down the track on our leading platoon screaming, *"kata! kata!"* ("hack! hack!"). Another group of terrorists, also screaming *"kata! kata!"*, ran up the track to attack our rear platoon. Although the majority of the terrorists were only armed with *pangas*, their numbers, their screaming and crazed, *bangi-(*cannabis-) induced charges, were hair-raising.

I couldn't see what was going on at either end of our patrol. My men had automatically left the track when we came under fire, and from their position, could blaze away at the enemy across the path. I ran forward to find Bramston. I found him terrified, cowering behind a fallen tree. He was in no state to give orders, so I raced back to my men. The enemy was withdrawing, so I ordered my platoon to cease fire. The company had driven off the enemy, suffering seven wounded. Enemy casualties were not recorded.

The outcome of this incident made me determined to avoid going again into action with Bramston. He had proved to be a cowardly, bungling soldier with little idea of how to mount a patrol. I had also confirmed my opinion that too large a number of men are not easy to control by hand signals in dense forest. After further experience, I limited my patrols to seven or eight men. By that time, there were no longer any attempts by the enemy to attack us in large numbers.

***

Bramston liked to take prisoners into the forest, from which they never returned. On more than one occasion he took an officer from Battalion HQ with him, so that the officer could notch the grip of his revolver by shooting a prisoner. I heard these horrific stories from disgusted brother soldiers, at least one of whom transferred out of the army to serve with the civil administration; such was his hatred of Bramston's behavior.

Capt. Mike Harris, the Company 2 i/c, ordered a Kenya Regiment Sergeant, Rick, to escort him when taking prisoners into a wooded valley. There Harris drove a thin bladed, double-edged Somali knife between a prisoner's ribs, and watched him die. Rick was sickened, but Harris wasn't finished. The next prisoner was shot from a couple of feet twice in his stomach with 9 mm rounds from a Patchett. Such were the prisoner's whimpering sobs of pain that the demented Rick shot him in the head in an act of mercy.

Then Harris dealt with a third, fettered, prisoner, by throwing a phosphorous grenade at him. These grenades cause the most terrible wounds, when burning phosphorous eats into flesh. Rick ran forward to help the prisoner, and was also burned. He threw the prisoner and himself into the river to expedite the burning of the phosphorous, and end the agony more quickly. The shrieking prisoner was so badly burned that Rick shot him in the head in another act of mercy. Harris was furious at Mick's actions, and threatened to shoot him in the stomach. But by now Rick was indifferent to what happened to him. He had killed unarmed prisoners, and his acts of mercy would certainly be questioned. He reported the events, but was deemed to have gone off his head, and was taken away for psychiatric treatment. We never saw Rick again.

Neither Bramston nor Harris was ever brought to justice for these murders, but one British officer from another unit was found guilty of murdering prisoners by shooting them in the back 'when attempting to escape'.

Capt. Griffiths, together with Sgt. Walker, took an 8 mm movie camera to record the killings. A prisoner was put in a hut while Griffiths and Walker stood outside on either side of the doorway. The prisoner was told to make a run for it, and if he made good his escape, he would be a free man. As the man raced out of the hut, Walker started filming, while Griffiths shot down the fleeing prisoner with his Patchett.

Griffiths was tried and sent back to the UK to serve a long term in the stockade, but Walker made his escape through Uganda and the Belgian Congo, never to return to Kenya.

I was convinced that some of the British officers seconded to the K.A.R. were considered second rate by their own regiments. Among the excellent British soldiers, there were wasters, alcoholics and cowards. I determined to avoid going into action with them.

It is certain that Idi Amin, the degenerate Ugandan president, was a product of the vile behavior. Surely, Sergeant Idi Amin, who served with A Company of the 4th K.A.R., learned his vicious ways from the murderous company commander, Major Bramston and his 2 i/c Captain Harris.

***

Idi Amin

The three platoons of A Company were ordered back to Company Headquarters and the Company Commander set about trying to gain information about the enemy in the forest. Now the whole Company was together, I was to meet some of the men from other platoons. One was a Sergeant Idi, later to become self-appointed Field Marshal Idi Amin Dada, the Ugandan tyrant, responsible for the deaths of at least half a million Ugandans.

I remember him as a very large man with a reputation as a heavyweight boxer. As was typical in the army, Idi's size and bearing, together with his physical prowess, led to his promotion to Sergeant. He had an air that big, strong men have, with confidence in their own ability to overpower ordinary mortals.

I saw him perform in a friendly boxing competition against a Kenya KAR battalion. His opponent was considerably lighter than Sgt. Idi, but was very fast on his feet and with his fists. He was confident he could out-box the heavier but slower Ugandan, until Sgt. Idi, in a pre-fight discussion, swore to kill and eat the lighter Kenyan. This, coming from the huge Ugandan, unnerved the contender who wanted nothing to do with a fighter from a tribe of reputed cannibals. The Kenyan entered the ring with a firm determination to put a stop to the fight as quickly as possible and went at Idi with a flurry of blows. These were effortlessly brushed aside, and the Ugandan won after he felled the Kenyan with one mighty blow born of sheer indignation. The terror stricken Kenyan scrambled from the ring with unseemly haste, happy not to be served up in a stew. Idi, ever cheerful, chortled at his opponent's discomfiture.

I remember Idi being willing to go on expeditions to Battalion Headquarters to collect rations, but I don't remember him being eager to go on patrol.

Not long before Uganda, a British Protectorate, was granted independence, the British government realized that something would have to be done about the formation of an African officer cadre. Sergeants and above were sent to England to attend a year long course at Sandhurst, the British Army's academy for officer training. It is said that every man passing out of Sandhurst has a Field Marshal's baton in his haversack. That is to say, he has the theoretical knowledge, if not the experience, necessary to be in overall command of armies. After Uganda independence, Idi was promoted to general, commanding the Ugandan army.

Idi Amin came from a small tribe of little political significance in Uganda. It was assumed that he would never be a threat to President Milton Obote, independent Uganda's first president. But the corrupt Obote had ruined the economy, and this was noted by the Ugandans. So, when Obote went to China to beg for funds in order to refill his pockets, and perhaps allow a few pennies to fall into the dust for the Ugandan Treasury, General Idi Amin staged a successful military coup d'etat. He promoted himself to the rank of Field Marshal, and awarded himself a breast full of medals for gallantry including the Victoria Cross.

Obote went to shelter in Tanzania with his friend President Julius Nyerere, who was busily ruining the Tanzanian economy with the 'benefits' of socialism. Nyerere was sincere, and was not engaged in lining his own pocket as Obote had done. Nyerere supported his deposed Ugandan colleague, and eventually helped him, by military action, to regain his position as President of Uganda.

Idi Amin found protection in Jeddah, Saudi Arabia, with Muslims who were happy to ignore atrocities carried out by one claiming to follow the Islamic faith.

9

Mau-Mau oaths

The Kikuyu tribe is renowned for the binding strength of their oaths. Tradition requires oaths be administered openly, and the rituals are innocuous, if mildly barbarous to Western eyes. In contrast, the depraved oaths administered covertly by the Mau-Mau broke with all decency. That they were binding, astonished anthropologists who had studied traditional Kikuyu oathing procedures and rites. Perhaps they were binding simply because the rituals were so degenerate.

To confer legitimacy, parts of the traditional rites were included. Banana leaves were formed into an arch through which the person taking the oath had to pass through seven times. Banana leaves and the number seven play a significant part in Kikuyu traditional oathing ceremonies, and other conventional rites were used by the Mau-Mau in order to affect a semblance of acceptable oathing conduct.

It is probable that few members of the tribe were intimately familiar with traditional oathing procedures, as oathing had long been stifled under British colonial administration, being deemed to be too frequently carried out under duress. But no doubt, most Kikuyu people had some idea of the old traditional ceremonies.

The Mau-Mau rituals included inserting the tail of a dog into the vagina of a menstruating woman. Those taking the oath were each required to lick it seven times while passing through an arch of banana leaves seven times as they chanted the oaths. They were also required to eat fingers and other body parts hacked from corpses.

Oaths varied, but usually included swearing to the following: To kill or to assist in the killing of a European and his family when ordered to do so; to flay, mutilate and dismember their victims' corpses; to hide anyone fleeing from the Security Forces; to steal from Europeans, including guns and ammunition and hand them over to the Mau-Mau; to keep secret all Mau-Mau affairs. Those who were induced to take Mau-Mau oaths would be killed, by the power of the oath, should they break any part of it.

Such was the strength of the oaths that the Security Forces introduced de-oathing ceremonies. These were fairly effective as they were held overtly, so those 'cleansed' made their renewed allegiance public. This took courage, although by the time this procedure was introduced, the Mau-Mau had become a weakened force.

For the first year or so, the terrorists were successful in slaughtering a number of settlers. They targeted Europeans with a reputation for helping Africans, and with sympathetic attitudes toward African aspirations. The terrorists could not allow such people to live, as their benevolence was contrary to Mau-Mau propaganda.

Two well known families, the Rucks and Micheljohns, were targeted for assassination as they had provided medical treatment for their employees and local villagers. When Mr and Doctor Ruck were attacked, Mr Ruck had gone out to treat a sick horse, and was the first to be slashed to death. Doctor Ruck went to find her husband and she too was hacked down, and her fetus ripped from her womb. Their young son was also slaughtered and their house ransacked.

The Michaeljohns suffered a similar fate.

Also murdered was the brother of the world famous anthropologist, Louis Leakey. Some of his body parts were used in oathing ceremonies. He was buried head down in the belief that this would prevent his soul from marching on.

When employers like the Rucks and Micheljohns were murdered, their employees were denied virtually free professional medical treatment. In the case of Leakey, the Kikuyu lost the sympathetic ear of a member of an influential family. The Leakeys had lived among the Kikuyu from the time they arrived in the colony, as missionaries, many years earlier. They were particularly well acquainted with the desires of the Kikuyu people, their language and customs.

Europeans living on isolated farms provided education and other benefits for their farm workers, in addition to medical treatment. Aged settlers, in particular, were targeted by the Mau-Mau. Some gangs gained admittance to farmhouses through the alleged treachery of long-serving Kikuyu employees. It was noted that all the bad traits, such as cowardice and treachery that old settlers had long attributed to the Kikuyu, seemed to be true.

However, the vast percentage of the Kikuyu were not willing Mau-Mau members. They and their families were under duress from the terrorists by threats of death if they failed to comply with orders. The Mau-Mau also knew the whereabouts of everyone's home in the Reserve. Therefore, families were also under threat if a reluctant recruit refused to submit to oathing and demands. The apparent treachery of loyal servants in abetting Mau-Mau gangs was, in many cases, almost certainly the result of these threats.

***

One incident occurred seven or eight miles from my platoon headquarters. We were camped in a disused warehouse. An earth road from the town of Thika ran past our camp, and continued up through the Abedare Range forest, the hideout of terrorists. Between our headquarters and Thika, there were several coffee plantations owned by Europeans. Security for the area was in the hands of the police. I was informed by radio from Company HQ that terrorists had attacked the owners of one of the estates.

I immediately set off with a section of my Ugandan soldiers in a truck. On arrival at the plantation I learned, from a policeman, something of what had happened. The plantation owners, an elderly couple, lived in one bungalow, while their daughter and son-in-law lived in another, a quarter of a mile away. The young couple, with their two children, had been to Thika to buy provisions. They returned to their bungalow after dark, and were unloading their purchases when flares from the other bungalow shot into the night sky. Leaving his wife and children, the son-in-law raced to his in-laws' house. Exactly what happened will never be known. The daughter waited for a phone call from her husband to tell her what had been going on. She waited in vain.

After trying for about an hour to reach her parents by phone, the daughter had phoned a neighbor and then the police. They discovered that the old couple and their son-in-law had been slashed to death, and then mutilated. Evidence indicated they had put up little resistance, hoping perhaps that the terrorists would take whatever they wanted and spare their lives. But it seemed that they had been slashed across their faces, heads and shoulders, and then butchered by decapitation. Their fingers had been severed and taken away, to be used in foul Mau-Mau oathing ceremonies. After assuring myself that the police and neighbors were in control, and looking after the grieving daughter and her children, I returned with my men to our camp.

When I returned to the scene of the outrage early the following day, I met the daughter and her two children. They had neighbors in attendance who told me the police had determined that, after slaughtering the old couple and their son-in-law, the terrorists had taken anything that took their fancy, then trashed the house and had tried, unsuccessfully, to set fire to it. I spent the day trying to determine in which direction the gang had made off. But the whole area was criss-crossed with the tracks of plantation workers, and I was unsuccessful in unraveling the entanglement. Police dogs had also been unable to follow the tracks. They had determined that the gang had started out in the direction of the forest.

Three weeks later, still hoping to come upon the gang or their tracks, I took a patrol into the forest, and found a terrorist camp, which we attacked. Although a sentry had seen us and had given the alarm, we managed to kill five of them, the rest racing off into the forest. Nightfall limited the time we had to carry out any follow-up, and we contented ourselves with a thorough search of the camp and the dead. A smoke-stained, silver George III tea-pot, hot water pot, milk jug and sugar bowl were discovered lying in the embers of a fire.

I took these to the woman whose husband and parents had been murdered. She immediately recognized them, and was pleased to get them back. She asked me how we had managed to find them, and was gratified to learn at least some of the gang had paid for the murders with their lives. She had spent each night after the incident either in sleeplessness or harrowing nightmares, in fear the Mau-Mau would return.

When I called again some days later to find out how she was managing to deal with the tragedy, and how her children were coping, I learned she had left Kenya. The plantation was being managed by a neighbor, pending the sale of the property. She felt that safety would never be a reality as long as there was one Mau-Mau left alive to find and murder her and her children.

***

The gang we had attacked was led by Mwangi Gadhe. They had suffered serious depredations from desertions, my sniping and our attacks. We learned from prisoners that, out of a gang numbering about 800, they had lost about 60 due to our actions. A considerable number had deserted, as their leader executed any member he mistrusted or who disobeyed his orders. Many more decided they did not, after all, want to be warriors and suffer hardship and perhaps death in the forest. The gang was now down to about thirty-five, and the prisoners told us the gang would now move, probably to the north. Mwangi Gadhe's harsh treatment of his gang led, a few weeks later, to his murder by members of his own gang.

***

I had proved small, well armed, patrols to be more likely to succeed. Three men carried short barreled .303 No. 5 Rifles each with a belt bandoleer of fifty rounds of ammunition. Three or four men, including myself, were armed with Patchetts with one magazine on the gun and four spare fully loaded magazines each holding thirty-four rounds. Another man carried a Bren and five magazines each loaded with twenty-five rounds. In addition, each of us carried extra ammunition for our own firearm and additional ammo for the Bren. Each man carried two fragmentation '36' grenades - designed to burst into thirty-six pieces of shrapnel when they exploded, - and two phosphorous grenades. And each man, excluding the Bren gunner, also carried a bayonet for his firearm.

One of our platoon commanders had to be rushed from a forest patrol to a military hospital. He was met by a sergeant who relieved him of his weapons and ammunition.

"Good heavens," exclaimed the sergeant, "You're a walking armory. You're carrying enough weaponry and ammo to start a full scale war all on you own".

The Mau-Mau had also determined big gangs were cumbersome, and difficult to control. A high percentage of their members didn't really support their cause, and hadn't the stomach for harsh life in the cold, wet mountains. Their gangs were becoming smaller as discontented deserters fled. Consequently, problems of feeding the gangs diminished. Fewer attention-attracting sorties had to be made to forage for food and supplies. The gangs of hard-core, experienced Mau-Mau became more mobile, and less easy to hunt down.

We now tried a new tactic. Each platoon commander took his men into the forest carrying as much as possible in provisions. My pack weighed 108 pounds, more than double the average. I carried extra ammunition and grenades, medical supplies, my own cooking utensils, and a camp stove with a bottle of oil. Once in the forest, a suitable place was found, and a semi-permanent camp established, from which section-strength local patrols were made. After a few days, the camp was moved.

The idea was to have patrols continuously in the forest, without having to cross the 'One Mile Area' where they could be seen by the terrorist observers in the forest fringe. Additional food supplies were air dropped. This didn't necessarily give the exact position of the platoon away, as it was difficult to see just where the drop landed, unless it was observed from very close by. But it did confirm there was a unit in the area. We always moved our base after a drop. The enemy, understandably, became very alert.

We had a skirmish deep in the forest with a small Mau-Mau gang, and we were able to take a prisoner. The prisoner was found hiding under a bank in water only a degree or so above freezing. The prisoner was brought to me shivering uncontrollably. He was chilled to the bone, and thought he was about to die.

I contacted our company HQ on the radio, and was told the Royal Air Force had been informed of the exact location of our encounter with the terrorists, and that the gang had fled northwards. The RAF was keen to bomb the area, and I was instructed to pull out of the forest.

I knew bombs had an awkward propensity to fall where they were not wanted. Hastily I assembled my men, and with the prisoner, we scurried out of the forest at great

Typical K.A.R. soldier ready for patrol.

speed. We covered nearly nine miles in an hour, despite being loaded down with heavy packs. Fortunately, our route was slightly downhill along a wide game trail.

The prisoner was handed over to the police after we had interrogated him. A month or so later he was brought to court on a charge of being found in a proscribed area, and of being a member of Mau-Mau. He would be hanged if found guilty of either charge.

Naturally enough, he lied, claiming I had captured him as he innocently walked past our camp down in the Kikuyu Reserve on his way to see his poor ailing mother. I did not appear in court, as I was elsewhere engaged in trying to hunt down his colleagues. Three men from my platoon, including the sergeant who had actually found the terrorist, gave evidence about the capture and where it took place.

The prisoner was judged to have been a reluctant Mau-Mau conscript, and was not hanged but sentenced to detention. My soldiers were disgusted with the claims made by the defense council and the outcome of the case. They told me no more prisoners would be taken. There was little I could do about this, though I did point out the necessity to take prisoners to try to elicit intelligence. During skirmishes in the forest I lost sight of some of my men. So I was not able to determine the circumstances in which a terrorist met his end.

My lecture about the importance of taking prisoners fell on deaf ears. I told our company commander about my men's attitude, but he shrugged saying there was little he could do about it. But he gave a talk to the whole company on the necessity to take prisoners. The men appeared indifferent.

Our forays into the forest were becoming less effective with fewer encounters with the enemy. The Mau-Mau gangs were smaller, and were now comprised of hard-core, experienced terrorists. A problem that still remained was any patrol heading into the forest had to pass through open farming areas of the Kikuyu Reserve. The terrorists could watch from vantage points within the forest edge, and determine a patrol's point of entry. It was decided we should build a permanent camp high up in the forest from where patrolling could be carried out unseen by the enemy.

There were several logging tracks leading into the forest. They followed permanent game trails, and since these were used by elephant, they tended to follow gentle climbs along the tops of ridges, skirting the steeper slopes. There was one disadvantage to this routing. The gentle slopes were not well drained, and the logging tracks and larger game trails became quagmires during rainy seasons. The logging tracks stopped where a belt of bamboo precluded the growth of trees. The game trails continued through the bamboo to a belt of high altitude forest, and went all the way up to the open moorlands at an altitude of 9,500 ft. above sea level.

We decided a permanent camp would have to be provisioned by trucks, and an all-weather road was necessary. If the bamboo was cut away, the track would dry out and remain passable in all seasons to four wheel drive vehicles.

Tony Swain, the most outstanding platoon commander in our unit, showed us how to clear bamboo. We employed 100 Kikuyu villagers, armed with their ubiquitous *pangas*, to cut back the bamboo about fifty paces on both sides of a major elephant trail. Tony's farming background provided him with experience in a wide range of practical activities. He spoke Swahili and had a working knowledge of Kikuyu. He tackled every task with vigor that inspired everyone to do his best.

***

"*Atiriri!*" (Kikuyu for "Pay attention!") Tony called, alerting our workforce of 100 Kikuyu. "We will divide into two equal teams. I will work with one team and my comrade, Lt. Gill, will supervise the other. Working in line abreast, with my team on one side of the track and his team on the other, we will give each and every bamboo one cut at waist level.

V.A.N. (TONY) SWAIN M.C.

Just hack once at each stem. Don't worry about those you don't cut through. Just carry on, hacking each stem once."

The Kikuyu workforce had never cleared bamboo in the way Tony instructed. The two teams advanced steadily giving each twenty-five foot high, four inch diameter stem a vigorous cut with a sharp *panga*. After covering about 150 paces, a gust of wind blew through the forest. A sound like the rattle of small arms fire alarmed all of us but Tony.

"*Kumbe!*" ("Crikey!"). Someone yelled.

"*Bunduki!*" ("Guns!").

"*Tunashambuliwa!*" ("We are being attacked").

"*Kaa kimya!*" ("Lie motionless!").

It was the bamboo falling. As those stems that had been cut fell near us, we had to run to avoid being hit and knocked down. After a couple of minutes, silence reigned.

Laughing, Tony called, "*Tudhie*" (Let's go).

Shamefaced at our interpretation of the rattling of the falling bamboo, we rose to our feet. Tony led us back to the beginning of the cut. We spread out line abreast on either side of the track again, to start clearing the fallen bamboo. This was quite an easy job as the stems lay more or less horizontal to the ground and downward strokes of the *pangas* sliced through the stems without difficulty.

The stems were cut into three foot lengths and left higgledy-piggledy to form a difficult-to-get-through, thirty inch deep, horizontal lattice. The idea was to afford protection to the track from the enemy, who would be wary of ambushing from close range. They would be unable to run off when the armed escorts on trucks returned fire.

The still standing bottom parts of the stems were about thirty inches high, and all that was necessary was to hack through the roots at the base of the stem at ground level. Using the piece of stem as a lever, it was broken from its roots. When the fallen bamboo was cleared off the track, we started on the next cut. This method of clearing allowed us to open up the track through the bamboo in record time.

We had to build a bridge. This was done by felling

suitable trees, manhandling the trunks across the stream, with smaller logs lying on them, followed by yet smaller branches, and finally stones and turf. Later, when the Royal Engineers came to improve our handiwork, they drove a Caterpillar D8 tractor over our bridge which proved capable of supporting the load.

***

Bamboo, of which there are several varieties, is a genus of giant tropical grass. The hollow, 'jointed' wooden stems taper from ground level. They may be 1¼" in diameter at the bases of the stems in the smaller varieties, to 4" in diameter in the case of the larger varieties. The stems vary in height from twelve to thirty feet. The 'joints' in the stems are nodes from which leafy stems grow. At each node the hollow stem is blocked by a woody disc, sealing each fourteen inch long inter-node at its top and bottom.

The smaller bamboo grows densely through which wild animals up to the size of rhino make narrow tunnels about 5 ft high. Patrolling in this type of bamboo required crouching, and was dangerous when a sleeping animal was awakened and raced down the tunnel. The bamboo could hide a sleeping animal barely two paces away. We might hear the rush of the startled animal, but were unable to get off the track where the bamboo grew too densely. A rhino could charge through the bamboo as easily as a human might run through long grass. We were unable to swing our weapons into action in the constricting bamboo.

I made a strict rule that no soldier was to open fire in dense bamboo as indiscriminate shooting could lead to hitting a comrade or further infuriating a panic stricken animal. More than one patrol suffered the charge of a startled rhino which knocked soldiers down. On one occasion the rhino stopped, and was trying to gore a fallen man when the patrol commander ran up, put his Patchett in the rhino's ear and fired a burst. Fortunately this killed the rhino and the soldier's life was saved.

On another occasion an inexperienced British officer fired a burst from his Patchett into a Kenya Regiment soldier from behind when a rhino charged down a tunnel. The Kenya Regiment soldier was hit several times but survived. The doctors had been worried about a bullet that had lodged in the soldier's lung, but the wounded man coughed up the bullet. Gratified, the doctors overlooked the seriousness of a wound in the thigh where an artery had been knocked into a vein. No blood was reaching the lower parts of the limb. The leg had to be amputated when gangrene set in.

The larger bamboo grew more sparsely and visibility was far better. But a charging elephant could smash his way through the bamboo which might knock a man down ten paces ahead of the elephant. On one occasion I was knocked down by a falling bamboo stem which had been shot away by a burst of enemy machine gun fire. I was more surprised than hurt, and it was several seconds before I realised I had not been wounded by a bullet.

***

Fort Essex

Having an all-weather track to the upper belt of trees, we now set about building a permanent camp at the top of a ridge. Two buildings were made from bamboo. Maj. Bramston, who had served with a Gurkha regiment in India, showed us how to make reasonably weatherproof buildings using this material.

A two acre flat area was cleared. Bamboo poles, sunk a foot into the ground, supported a framework of stout bamboo columns lashed with horizontal cross and diagonal members. Rafters were also of bamboo poles wired to vertical columns of several bamboo poles, also bound together with wire. We used no nails, only barbed wire of which we had a plentiful supply.

Bamboo stems, 4 in. diameter, were cut into 9 ft. lengths for walls or 14 ft. lengths for roofs. Each piece was split in half lengthwise, and the node discs were cut out. By arranging a roof of split lengths side by side as a series of channels, and then covering the gaps between with inverted bamboo in the manner of Spanish or Roman tiles, a weatherproof roof was formed. Walls were of similar construction.

One building was a dormitory/cookhouse for the men, and the other provided sleeping quarters, cookhouse and an office for the officers. We dug latrine pits, and erected bamboo huts over them.

Trenches were dug around the buildings to form a defensive circle against possible attack. An earth embankment was raised all round the camp with a 10 ft. wide, 10 ft deep trench outside, modeled on the defenses built in Roman times some 2,000 years ago. Our fortifications were elephant proof. A double barbed wire fence on top of the embankment completed our defenses.

Undoubtedly the enemy knew about Fort Essex, named after the Company Commander's English county regiment, but it was never attacked. We were able to patrol from the camp without having to trek through open farmland before reaching enemy occupied forest areas. This led to a number of successes and, eventually, the whole area was denied to the terrorists who decamped to safer territory.

The Kenya Police Air Wing

One of the more successful arms of the security forces operating against the Mau-Mau was the Kenya Police Air Wing. The pilots were, in the main, very experienced 'bush pilots' who knew the country well. They flew light aircraft - 4 seaters - and were able to drop supplies to patrols on the ground, spot fleeing gangsters, and help patrols to determine their exact location. Communication from ground to aircraft was by VHF radio. In the forest, where it was usually not possible to see more than about 50 yards, map reading was difficult. The maps were not always accurate, and while it was usually possible to be sure that a patrol had reached one of the larger rivers, it was difficult to tell how far up the river they were. Many small tributaries were not marked on the maps, but some were, and this led to further confusion. Even experienced patrol commanders were lucky if they were able to say, with certainty, where they were within about 1,000 yards.

The Air Wing pilots were generally very patient with patrol commanders. A plane could not be seen by someone standing in a forest until it was virtually overhead, so those on the ground had to guide the pilot by the sound of the aircraft's engine. Very rarely could the pilot hope to see the patrol as the forest was too dense. Even if the patrol was in a clearing, the pilot had his hands full in flying the light aircraft over the hilly, tree covered ground through dangerous, ever changing up- and down-draughts. And patrol commanders were not always helpful. One patrol commander tried to direct a pilot over the radio.

"I'm standing at the foot of a tree," he explained. "Can you see me?"

"I can see about 1,000 trees," spluttered the pilot. "Can you be a bit more explicit?"

"Well, it's a big tree with green leaves. I can see you. Can't you see me?"

"No. Could you possibly climb to the top of the tree and wave?"

"It's very tall and the branches are all near the top. I don't think I can manage to climb it. But wait a moment.............I'm waving with my handkerchief. It's white. Can you see me now?"

"No."

"Can you suggest anything else?"

"No. But your map reference is ...." The pilot gave a six figure map reference, and then continued. "I suggest when you next go to Nairobi you contact the Kenya Police Air Wing HQ, and ask to be taken over the forest in a plane to see the forest from the air. You might then understand why I find it difficult to see you standing at the foot of a tree."

"Oh! What a good idea! Yes, I'll do that. Can you give me that map reference again? I'll write it down. Oh! My pencil's broken. Can you hang on a moment?"

"No!" The pilot flew off.

***

We took our hats off to the pilots who we rarely had any chance of meeting. The pilots realised that the poor guys on the ground were to spend night after night in the cold, wet forests, while the pilots were able to tumble into warm beds. So there was mutual respect, and when we did meet up with the pilots, a merry time followed. The pilots could drink us under the table. They had plenty of practice whilst we slogged around in the forests.

Two of the best known Air Wing pilots were invited to a colleague's wedding in Nairobi, where they enjoyed a glass or eight of innocuous looking Champagne. Afterwards, they had to fly up to their airfield, an hour's flight away. They had to make this journey in daylight, as the airfield had no landing-strip lights or any other landing aids. The two pilots wove their way to the light aircraft airport in Nairobi, installed themselves in the plane, and took off.

"That was a pretty poor take-off, Timber" muttered Punch.

"Too bloody right," retorted Timber. "I thought you to be a better pilot."

"Well, it's you who's flying this wretched machine," said Punch.

"No I'm not. You are."

"I am NOT!" yelled Punch. "You are."

"You are in the left hand seat, so you are flying this

airplane. So it was you who did that awful take-off," argued Timber.

"I may be sitting in the left hand seat, but you are flying the machine." Punch was adamant.

"I am NOT. You took off and you are flying her!" Timber was equally adamant. The argument continued for a further few seconds before the plane landed itself in the Nairobi Game Park, a mile from the airfield. There was no damage. By some miracle the plane had missed hitting any rocks or thorn trees.

"Now look what you've done!" sighed Punch.

"Quite a good landing though," remarked Timber.

"You'd better walk over to the office and tell them what you've done," suggested Punch, who was damned if he was going walk through lion country to admit that it was he who had nearly spoiled one of the Police Air Wing Cessnas.

At this moment a Land Rover drove up, and the two tipsy pilots were taken away, while a colleague looked into the question of flying the airplane back to the airfield, before the Commissioner of Police found out about the short flight that two of the most experienced Air Wing pilots had executed with such finesse.

***

We were allowed a forty-eight hour furlough every month. On one occasion I went with our company second-in-command, Mike Harris, into Nairobi. On the way we stopped for lunch at a roadside hotel, and met a bunch of Kenya Police Air Wing lads with whom we 'got involved' out on a patio. Beer flowed, and we were having a good time. I booked us into the hotel as I could foresee we would be in no condition to continue our drive into Nairobi.

As is usual where there are young pilots, there were several girls enjoying the party. The reason young, active-service pilots attract girls has little to do with their good looks or intelligence. It is simply because they are available.

We poor infantry soldiers were stuck out in the forest in rain and cold, but pilots nearly always make it back to a warm, comfortable billet - and so to bed..............

The availability of eager girls hardens pilots, who become pretty off-hand in their attitude to the young lovelies who bestow their favors on them. Apparently one young lady, who had fallen for a couldn't-care-less pilot, felt she was being ignored. After a few sharp words, she stormed off. I was tempted to follow to console her, but I had a full tankard of cold beer on the table in front of me, and this seemed to be of greater importance. After some minutes there was the sound of a shot from a second floor bedroom window. Several of our party rushed off to investigate, but not the pilot for whom the girl pined. Moments later a young pilot hurried back to report.

"The silly little bitch has shot herself in the head. She's bleeding like hell."

"Well tie a tourniquet tightly round her bloody neck," snapped the girl's cavalier. "Unless anyone knows of another method of staunching blood streaming from a head wound," he added, perhaps feeling his suggested treatment sounded a little too insensitive.

I have to admit I found his attitude amusing, as did most of the tipsy company around the table. Surely it was the beer that made us unmindful of the girl's predicament and distress. I am pleased to report she had taken some care not to shoot herself through the head. The bullet had caused a scalp wound, and though it bled a lot and caused a severe headache, it also knocked some sense into her. She made a full recovery, dropped her lust for pilots, and became attached to a dashing young Kenya Regiment soldier who was more gallant.

10

Remarkable brothers

In the area for which we were responsible there was a remarkable Kikuyu family. There were three brothers. The eldest, Samwel Kimemia, owned a transport company and general stores in surrounding villages. His younger brother William Kimemia was a leading school teacher. The third and youngest brother, Paul Kimemia, was an easily-led layabout.

Samwel and William were regarded as outstanding leaders in their community, and behaved as responsible role models. They regarded Paul as a vulnerable, weak link in the family chain. Perhaps they were not surprised when they learned Paul had taken the Mau-Mau oath. They apprehended and severely punished him. Thereafter Paul was watched over closely. He was given no freedom and had to carry out only the most humiliating duties. He was treated as a shameful, worthless creature, deserving no respect.

We needed local collaboration in our anti-Mau-Mau activities, but anyone seen to be helping us put his life in jeopardy. One day Samwel turned up at our base, and had a long conversation with the Major. We were not to know the outcome of this conversation until some six weeks later when a Mau-Mau came to the gates of our base, and asked to see the officer-in-charge. He was taken at gun point to see the Major who, after a couple of hours, called the platoon commanders into his office tent. Sitting at ease was a dirty, smelly, bearded ruffian in a ragged overcoat and rubber soled half-boots, typical of Mau-Mau terrorists. We were taken aback as the brute was smiling broadly. One by one our jaws dropped as we recognized Samwel.

When we heard his story, we realized just how brave this man was. On his previous visit, he had persuaded the Major to let him have a Sten sub-machine gun and a quantity of ammunition. The Sten had a magazine that could be charged with up to twenty-five 9mm rounds. At short range it was a useful weapon. The butt was removable so the weapon could be concealed under an overcoat.

It had been agreed that Samwel go around the local area, posing as a Mau-Mau terrorist. He had located those who were willing to actively help the terrorists in the acquisition of food and medicines. He had actually been in contact with terrorists in the forest, claiming to have come from a gang operating further north.

By degrees, he had built up a considerable amount of information about the gangs, where their camps were, where they obtained food, clothing and medical supplies, and who their leaders were. From this information, nineteen local Mau-Mau supporters were arrested by District Officer Thomson, and all the food that had been bagged, ready to be carried away by the terrorists, was confiscated. The nineteen terrorists were individually interrogated at great length by Samwel's brother William, until every drop of information they had to give was squeezed out of them. They were then handed over to the police, charged, taken before a court, convicted and hanged in accordance with the law.

William became our chief interrogator, a job at which he was brilliant. If a prisoner was taken, it was important he be questioned, and persuaded to give information well within 24 hours. The gang would move if a man went missing for that period. Therefore, it was imperative we act promptly on the information extracted.

William affected a pretense to be a friend with sympathy for Mau-Mau aims. He showed understanding of the usual claim the prisoner really had no information to give as he was only an assistant to the cook. William let the prisoner believe he had influence over us. As long as good information was made available to William, he would be able to make up a cover story for the prisoner that would be acceptable to us, and the prisoner would be freed. Once the prisoner began to talk, he was lost. William would go over and over the story, until the prisoner became tired. If he had lied, William would turn on him, saying he would not be able to help if the prisoner continued to lie, and tried to make a fool of his interrogator.

It would take him up to twelve hours to get the full true story from a prisoner, but every prisoner William interrogated ended up spilling the beans. His patience was amazing. After interrogation, prisoners were handed over to the civil administration, and District Officer Thomson arranged for their trials. We now had a very comprehensive picture about the terrorist gangs in the forest and faced the problem of how best to attack them.

The Kimemia brothers survived the Mau-Mau rebellion. Even Paul, after a period when he was treated as a slave by his brothers, became as useful member of society. Surprisingly, none of the brothers wanted to assume higher responsibility after the rebellion. They remained active, popular examples of good citizenship.

11

Davo, a great fighter and teller of tales

One day a heavily bearded man walked into our camp accompanied by his 'Man Friday', a Masai tribesman who acted as a scout. Davo, to give him the nick-name he used, told many tales of his past, and I was to hear them over and over again. Each time they differed. What he told me was this: David O. Davidson, or was it David O'Davidson, was born, sometime around 1900, in Scotland When still a young boy, his family moved to Australia. He claimed he had to depart hurriedly from Queensland just ahead of the Australian police for sheep stealing. He embarked on a cargo boat as a crew member, and jumped ship in South America.

According to Davo, he joined a band of Bolivian gangsters, and had been involved in social banditry, holding up transporters of payrolls, banks and any other custodians of large sums. Most of the booty went to finance political dissidents seeking to overthrow the government. After learning as much as he could about gangsterism, Davo made his way into the United States. There he joined gangs holding up the payrolls of oil well drillers and operators in Texas. So successful was his gang that they were offered the job of protecting the payrolls.

Davo alleged that in the late twenties, he made his

way up to Chicago where he joined Al Capone in his booze running operations, and became one of Capone's personal protectors. He claimed one day the cops surrounded Capone's hideaway, and Capone ordered him to see if there was an escape route out of the back of the building. When Davo opened a door in the rear wall of the backyard, a G-man was there to greet him with a burst from a Thompson's machine gun. Davo was hit nine times straight up the middle of his belly and chest, but survived.

He was advised to leave America after a long convalescence in a Federal 'hotel'. In 1937, he found himself fighting in the Spanish Civil War, which, with some help from Hemingway, he won. Hemingway may not have known it, but he and Davo were great buddies. Davo claimed a world record. He told us he shot and killed a man at 240 paces with a .45 caliber revolver.

After that adventure, he joined the British Army and served with East African troops during WWII. He was discharged honorably, and took the job of a District Officer in the White Highlands, where he gained the reputation for fair, summary justice. If an African came to him complaining that his employer had hit him, Davo would go immediately to question the employer. If the employer admitted the offense, he was asked why he had hit the man. If it was because the man had annoyed him on some trivial matter, Davo would deal the employer a heavy blow.

Davo was a short, thick-set man who had many unarmed combat skills, and could hit sensitive areas very hard. If the employer had hit the man for not obeying instructions leading to damage or loss, Davo gave the employee a knuckle sandwich for bothering him. Davo always insisted on sufficient evidence and/or corroboration before doling out summary justice. He was popular with everyone including his seniors, as minor cases were handled quickly and effectively. Few wished to bring further complaints to him unless they were genuine.

Davo neither smoked nor drank, and kept away from

DAVO DAVIDSON

bars and places where macho types might wish to provoke him into fights. This would have been very silly as Davo was an accomplished fighter, capable of using all manner of street fighting tricks, and he would have been very difficult to beat.

After a period in the Colonial Administration, Davo obtained employment as an overseer on a farm owned by a woman in the north western foothills of the Aberdare Range, an area that was to come under continual attack by the terrorists. There Davo found it prudent and necessary to continue daily target practice, firing up to 300 rounds a day. Since the cost of ammunition was an obvious factor, he used twin .22" caliber revolvers of similar weight and balance as his .38" caliber weapons.

Certainly Davo was a superb marksman, and demonstrated his skills with revolvers, sub-machine guns, rifles and Brens, shooting accurately, from the hip, at targets up to a range of seventy paces. A favorite trick was to toss a coin into the air above his right shoulder, draw his revolver and shoot the coin. Success was evinced when the bullet whined away and the bent coin was passed around the admiring audience.

He once demonstrated his unarmed combat skills, using me as his foe. I had to go for him with a knife as though to jab an additional navel in his guts. I found myself sailing through the air in a graceful arc, but I cannot claim to have landed elegantly. Had I not anticipated Davo's intention, I'd have suffered a dislocated elbow. I had gone at him with the knife in my left hand, hoping this might give me the slight advantage of surprise. I was wrong. I was nursing an injured arm, and was incensed that Davo should have thrown me without first determining how I might save myself from more serious injury. All I had been able to do was to assist my flight over Davo's shoulder by lifting off with my toes.

Davo came to where I lay in the dust trying to orient myself, my teeth, eyes and sundry other parts, which seemed to have become dislodged from their usual places. He asked if I was OK, and apologized for having been a bit stupid, and congratulated me on avoiding serious injury. This was an unjustified assumption if the level of pain was any indication. So, I bit my lip, held back my rage, and bravely muttered "Oh, that's all right old boy," in the spirit of a courageous English sportsman after someone had hit him, accidentally, with a cricket bat.

The day Davo arrived at our camp after coming through the Aberdare Range forest with his Masai 'Man Friday', he claimed to have seen a very large gang. He said he had seen lean-to sheds with corrugated iron roofs and women seamstresses at work with Singer treadle-operated sewing machines making warm clothing. Davo wanted us to accompany him immediately to attack the terrorist camp. But our company commander had to contact Battalion HQ to get permission from the Colonel for a raid into the forest. We had to wait for several days for the Colonel to get through to Brigade Headquarters, who then had to get onto General Headquarters in Nairobi, to get the necessary permission. Davo fumed with impatience at the delay.

I too was impatient, and I was sure permission to enter the forest would take time. I returned to my platoon base, leaving Davo at our company headquarters. I entered the forest with my platoon without permission. We started out at 2:00 a.m., and made our way as quietly as possible into the forest. Our concern for silence didn't really matter, as it was raining very heavily, and the noise of the storm drowned all other sounds. After entering the forest we halted, and waited for sunrise as it was too dark to proceed.

At dawn we advanced in single file along a wide elephant trail. It was all too easy to use wide game trails. We were able to advance quickly and quietly, and could see up to 300 ft. ahead. However, the terrorists could see us.

We were making our way diagonally up the side of a ridge, when we came under fire. We opened up on where we supposed the enemy to be. I had emptied the magazine of my sub-machine gun into the bushes, and was replacing it when a terrorist sprang from behind a tree some six feet from me with a *panga* raised above his head. I dropped the sub-machine gun magazine, drew my .455 Colt revolver, raised it and fired at the terrorist. I saw his clenched teeth disappear when my shot smashed into them. He was thrown back, dead before his body hit the ground. The whole action had taken but a few minutes. The rest of the gang ran away and all firing ceased.

An apparition visits Mum

Three weeks after the incident, I went home on a forty-eight hour furlough to be greeted by Mum who asked, "What happened to you?"

"What do you mean, what happened to me?" I asked.

"Well, you came home three weeks ago, never said a word, and left again."

"What do you mean?"

Mum told me she had been making jam tarts in the pantry when she heard a car coming up the road. The car slowed and turned into the yard. Mum saw my car pass by a window and stop in the drive. Moments later she heard the car door shut, the front door of the house open and close, and the sound of my army boots as I walked along the corridor leading to my bedroom. Mum wiped her hands, and came through to my room where I stood with my back to the door, emptying my pack onto the bed.

"Hello," said Mum to which she received no reply. She thought I was absorbed in dealing with the contents of my pack. "Come through to the pantry when you've finished," she said, and left me to get on with whatever I was doing.

She returned to the pantry, and after a few minutes heard my footsteps coming down the corridor. The front door opened and closed, the gravel crunched as I crossed the drive, my car door slammed, and I drove away. She assumed

I had rushed off to get something from the shops a couple of miles away. But I didn't return, and Mum was left baffled, until I arrived three weeks later.

I worked out the date and time which coincided exactly with the moment my life was in peril from a *panga-*wielding terrorist. I was actually in the midst of the ambush when Mum thought I visited home. I was not thinking of my mother or of home at that time, being too absorbed in saving my life.

I do not believe in the occult. I do not know how to explain Mum's strange experience, how or why it could have occurred. Mum was adamant that it happened.

Back to Davo and cold, wet reality

After our foray into the forest, we returned to our platoon base to await events. Permission finally came through from General Headquarters in Nairobi for us to enter the forest in company strength: about eighty-five men. We were ambushed and suffered casualties, one of which was Davo. He was shot twice in the stomach by a terrorist lying in the undergrowth, aiming carefully with a chromium plated .38" caliber 'Police Special'. Davo was wearing a bullet proof vest, and the bullets hit this as Davo was running bent forward. Two bullets hit the vest and were deflected low into Davo's stomach.

A Kenya Regiment Sergeant, Paddy Hewett, saw Davo go down. Ignoring enemy fire, he ran forward to see a revolver glinting in the fist of a terrorist in the undergrowth. He poured bursts from his Patchett at this target. Davo tried to get up, and the terrorist shot him again, this time in the thigh. Paddy continued to fire at the terrorist, who continued to fire at Davo who was again hit in the thigh. Finally the terrorist succumbed to Paddy's accurate fire. After the action we found that the terrorist had been hit in his back and shoulders twenty-four times as he lay prone in the undergrowth.

Davo again struggled to his feet, only to find his treasured Beretta 9 mm sub-machine gun had jammed. He ran forward to engage the enemy with the butt of his gun. At this moment he was hit through his right hand by a shot from a Bren fired by another gang member who was determined to end Davo's days. The .303 round also smashed the butt of his Beretta. Davo fell again. This time he didn't get up.

The Mau-Mau withdrew and Davo was carried on a make-shift stretcher after he had been given a morphine injection which, together with his wounds and loss of blood, put him out. This was fortuitous, as the patrol was again ambushed, and Davo was dropped by the stretcher bearers when they felt it prudent to take cover.

Davo never knew of this second ambush, and after making a full recovery, narrated the tale of his wounding many times, each yarn differing somewhat from the others. He claimed the Mau-Mau knew of his prowess at fighting, and he was their main target that day. In light of the number of times he was hit, this claim may have been justified. However, it is difficult to understand how the terrorists knew Davo was accompanying the patrol or how they recognized him. More probably, it was he who was hit first, and when he went down the enemy were determined to finish him off. But Davo had proved how difficult it was to kill him, and how determined he was to fight back, even when wounded. The patrol reached the forest edge. Davo was given medical attention, and was then rushed off to a Nairobi hospital.

When the Mau-Mau scattered after the second ambush, mortar fire was laid down in the direction from which the fleeing terrorists were shouting, whistling and sounding rallying bugle calls. The enemy was reforming, possibly with the aim of carrying out another attack. But the mortar fire was apparently accurate, since the shouts and bugle calls suddenly ceased.

No dead terrorists had been found close to the

second ambush. Some of our men said that they had seen enemy hit, but their firearms were attached with cord to comrades who ran off dragging the difficult-to-replace weapons. They were followed by their struggling wounded

The following evening morale was raised by the news that a sister company had found some seventy dead Mau-Mau terrorists, killed by mortar fire. This was difficult to believe, but it was reported that the mortar bombs had exploded in the branches of trees with devastating effect on the enemy below.

Many subsequent patrols into the forest failed to find any evidence of the enemy camp with corrugated iron roofed shelters and Singer sewing machines, which Davo had claimed to have seen.

12

Man on the run

There had been a number of Kikuyu men hiding in the forest for many years before the Mau-Mau Rebellion. They lived by trapping and honey hunting. Most were fleeing from the law, and most of them found sympathetic supporters in the adjacent Kikuyu Reserve. They were able to supply honey, game meat, and even trout from the mountain streams in exchange for other food and supplies. They knew the forest well, and had been forced to join Mau-Mau gangs as guides.

I captured one of these men who had been in the forest for some seven years. Kinanjui had gone into Nairobi job seeking. On his first full day there, he had become involved with some men who said they'd help to find work for him the following morning. That night they were joined by others, and a beer party ensued. A quarrel developed, and an oil lamp was knocked over. When it was re-lit, a corpse lay on the floor with a knife sticking out of him.

Everyone fled, and Kinanjui managed to make his way thirty miles to the forest near his home. There he stayed, assuming the police were after him. He was convinced they would consider him to be the murderer, simply because he had been a stranger at the beer party. I took my emaciated captive to the local headman, who recognized him. Enquiries were made. It turned out Kinanjui had never been wanted by the police, who had solved the murder within a day or so. The poor fugitive had lived alone in the forest all those years under a misapprehension. He was warmly welcomed by his village, and seemed unduly grateful to me for getting his life sorted out. He married a few months later, and I hope lived happily ever after.

***

One night we had a visit from the District Officer in charge of the local Kikuyu Guard posts. He told us he had information that a Kikuyu Guard post near our company base was to be attacked by terrorists. A platoon was sent to check the trenches within the fence were usable, to check if the walls had fallen in, that the 10 ft. wide, 10 ft deep dry moat surrounding the compound was in good condition, and the *'panjies'* had not fallen to the bottom of the trench. *Panjies* are eighteen inch long stakes sharpened at both ends. One end of each was pushed into the wall or bottom of the moat, so they bristled like a porcupine, making any attempt to jump into the moat perilous indeed.

The barbed wire fences were checked and the coils of barbed wire between the double fences were also inspected. Every Kikuyu Guard's (KG's) shotgun was inspected and tested, and ammunition was checked. Each armed KG had 50 rounds of 12 gauge buckshot cartridges. These fired nine ¼ inch balls, and were lethal at a range of up to fifty feet. The presence of our platoon did much to raise the morale of the KG. It was thought the terrorists would not attack that night, as there had been so much activity in the post, so the platoon was withdrawn. My platoon took up position, after dark, the following evening.

I made sure my men were properly deployed about

the post along with their comrades-in-arms, the KG. I checked the drawbridge and gate, and we settled down to a sleepless night. I heard movements outside the fence, and alerted the already watchful force. Suddenly we were fired on from two different directions. We held our fire, and the terrorists charged, supposing the KG to be too scared by the attack to return fire. The leading terrorists were carrying poles with which they tried to sweep away the *panjies* in the moat. They had little success in the dark. The remainder of the enemy surged impatiently behind the sweepers. The post was surrounded by some 800 terrorists, we were later informed.

On my order, all our men opened up on the enemy, who were cut down by a withering fire from Brens, Patchetts, rifles and shotguns. I fired flares into the air, and saw groups of enemy fall in a hail of fire which went on for several minutes. To make our attackers think reinforcements had arrived, I hurled hand grenades to land and explode behind the enemy as they crowded in screaming groups preparing to breach our defenses. When we could detect no further movement from the enemy, the KG wanted to let down the drawbridge to go out to finish off the wounded. I refused, as apart from anything else, we had no idea how far the enemy had withdrawn.

We stayed alert for the rest of the night. Occasionally someone would let off a burst of LMG or Patchett fire at some sound outside the wire. Some of the noises were the gurgles or death-rattles of the dying, or sobs or groans from the wounded. But other sounds were possibly hyenas and jackals attracted by the scent of blood. At daybreak I took a section out to look for wounded, arms and ammunition. Bodies lay everywhere. Some were lying in the moat pierced by the *panjies*. Others were hanging on the outer fence where they had been shot from less than ten paces as they attempted to climb through or over the barbed wire. Still more had obviously escaped.

✳✳✳

As I completed my tour round the post, I spotted someone crawling into a clump of bracken. I shouted at him to lie still, and a soldier ran to take him prisoner. He was in a confused state. This we put down to *bangi* (cannabis) the enemy often used to bolster their courage. Under the influence of *bangi*, the terrorists had, on several occasions, charged into a hail of fire which there was no hope of overcoming.

The prisoner had difficulty speaking, and seemed to find it impossible to stay awake. His eyes rolled and his head fell sideways. I had him led staggering into the guard post to a lockable cell where he passed out for several hours. Twenty armed Kikuyu Guard went out to follow the fleeing gang. They came upon dead and wounded terrorists, but the remainder of the gang had escaped into the forest where the KG was banned from following. Their single barreled shotguns were deemed to be inadequate for jungle warfare.

When he came to, I questioned the prisoner. Kinanjui had been employed by a Mrs Kent, whom I knew, as her gardener on the western slopes of the Aberdare Range. He was an epileptic, and had suffered a fit when the shooting started. He had come to, stiff and cold, suffering from a terrible headache, to find dead bodies all around him. He didn't know where he was, and could remember little. A mug of tea was brought, and I gave him a couple of aspirins from my first-aid pouch.

The KG went out to search the bodies, and the District Officer was called up on the radio to arrange for finger printing of the dead and their burial. My platoon, with the prisoner, went back to our company base. Over the course of the next few days, it became apparent that Kinanjui, an immensely strong man, had been taken by the Mau-Mau at night from Mrs. Kent's farm, and conscripted into the gang as a cook. Clearly he had no sympathy for the Mau-Mau cause, and wanted only to be left alone to work in the garden he lovingly tended for his employer.

He was a simple fellow, and since it wasn't possible for me to return him to his employer, I engaged him as a servant. For a year or so, during which Kinanjui became a stalwart aide, he laundered my clothes, kept my tent clean and tidy, acted as an interpreter, and earned a regular wage. He felt indebted to me, his benefactor, and encouraged me to learn Kikuyu. But too often I was away on patrol, and was a sporadic and incompetent student, despite his enthusiastic tutoring. When we were posted to another area, he joined the KG. Years later, after I had returned to civilian life, I met Mrs Kent, and told her the story of how an epileptic fit had saved her ex-gardener from death. I was gratified to learn he had returned to her employ when the Emergency ended. I was never censured for giving sanctuary to an ex-member of Mau-Mau.

***

Information indicated the Mau-Mau gangs were still losing members, and were short of ammunition. Many of them were suffering from edema from living out in the open at high altitude in cold, wet conditions. Smoke from wood fires brought on coughing fits. Food was frequently in short supply, and there were no facilities for treating the sick and wounded, many of whom died. Any dissatisfaction with gang leaders that arose among the terrorists was put down extremely harshly, often by execution. Desertion from the Mau-Mau gangs continued. Gang members had to be very committed to the Mau-Mau cause to put up with such conditions and treatment. Those that did stay with the gangs in the forests were really hard-core fanatics.

A Senior Chief takes action

In the area for which our company was responsible

there was a Senior Chief of the Kikuyu, Njiri, a highly respected man. He was loyal to his people, and was willing to follow colonial government policies if he deemed they were beneficial. Such was the esteem in which he was held by the colonial authorities, that he had been awarded the British Empire Medal. He usually wore a blanket over one shoulder with his B.E.M. pinned to it. He was a tall man, and his portly figure stood out among his people, who tend to be short in stature. Njiri was a no-nonsense, autocratic administrator of justice, and this was much appreciated by Africans, who tire of the ponderous management of legal procedures that is the wont of British colonial administration.

Senior Chief Njiri had a blind spot. One of his sons, Thigiru, was a worthless, two faced schemer. Njiri could see no wrong in the young man, and became choleric if anyone tried to draw attention to Thigiru's failings. Knowing that, in the eyes of his powerful father, he could do no wrong, Thigiru, by devious and underhand means, gained wealth and power. But Thigiru also gained enemies, who had to bide their time before making efforts to end his rapacity.

Njiri had his *boma* (stockade) on Kinyona Ridge. Immediately to the north was the Erati River, and north of that was the Erati Ridge. Njiri instructed Thigiru to build a Kikuyu Guard Post on Erati Ridge. Vacant school buildings were to provide the headquarters of the Guard Post. Njiri's *boma* had been fortified with a *panji* filled dry moat, double barbed wire fences, draw bridge and trenches like all Kikuyu Guard posts. Thigiru was to adopt the same general design for the Erati Ridge KG post. Thigiru would become the headman of the post, and looked forward to conducting his nefarious affairs with greater freedom in isolation from his father.

The construction of the post was a lengthy job, entailing the building of additional accommodation, and the erection of defenses. Thigiru and his construction team marched daily from Kinyona Ridge, down into the Erati

River Valley and up to the crest of the Erati Ridge. Each evening the team returned to Njiri's *boma* by the same route.

In time, Thigiru became overconfident and more arrogant. He had friends in the terrorist gangs whom he helped when occasion presented itself - by giving sanctuary, alibis, or character reports when a terrorist was captured. Thigiru had so many *fatinas* (feuds) that he began to have difficulty in deciding how to treat some terrorists. The Mau-Mau attitude was that anyone acting in any way against a member was, *ipso facto*, an enemy of Mau-Mau. Exactly what happened is not known. It was said Thigiru decided to end a *fatina*, and took terminal action against a Mau-Mau terrorist. He was ambushed by the deceased's comrades one evening in the Erati River Valley when returning to his father's *boma*. He and his immediate strong-arm escort were killed.

Had Njiri known of Thigiru's Mau-Mau connections, he would have exploded. But now he was devastated by the death of his favorite son. His grief soon turned to rage. He took a well-armed patrol along Kinyona Ridge, through the 'One Mile Area' up to the forest edge. There he crossed the Erati River Valley to the Erati Ridge, where he spread his men out across the ridge, and swept down for some ten miles.

Outside every hut were sacks of food, with head straps tied round them ready to be carried up to the forest for the terrorists. Tracks along the Erati Ridge showed constant use by the terrorists. Njiri returned to his *boma* by way of the Erati River Valley where, again, he found food ready to be borne away, and more tracks indicating regular use by the forest gangs.

Over the next two days Njiri took a large squad of armed KG, first down the Erati Ridge and then down the Erati River Valley. Every living creature was shot and killed - about 225 men, women and children on the ridge and about 175 in the valley. This he did entirely on his own authority.

We heard about it two days later, and were shocked. Our Company Commander, Major John Bramston, took a

Land Rover with me and a fellow Kenya Regiment Sergeant up to the area. Before going to see Njiri, we drove across the Erati River Valley and up onto the ridge. We had to drive round bodies left lying everywhere. Not only did we see human corpses, we saw dead donkeys, cows, goats, sheep, dogs and chickens. Nothing moved. The stench of death permeated everything.

We returned to Njiri's *boma*, and Bramston went in to see the Senior Chief. What was said, I don't know. A loyal and respected Senior Chief was responsible for an atrocity, but there was plenty of evidence that the people in the valley and on the ridge had been aiding and abetting the enemy. Njiri had put the colonial administration in a serious dilemma. I never heard what, if any, measures were taken against the resolute and esteemed Senior Chief. The massacre didn't diminish his standing among his people.

The following day Bramston took Tony Swain, me and a well armed squad with a 3 inch mortar in a truck up onto Erati Ridge. About 100 yards from the forest edge the vehicle stopped, the squad spread out, and several mortar bombs were fired to land a couple of hundred yards inside the forest. Almost immediately, terrorists fled from the forest toward our waiting squad. Presumably the enemy thought they were being attacked from behind by a force in the forest. They were cut down by our fusillade. Then we charged up to the forest edge, spread out and swept back down the ridge picking off any terrorists crouching in the long grass. This action, and the number of terrorists we killed, gave strength to the Senior Chief's contention that the whole area constituted refuge for a large Mau-Mau gang. It was generally held that the gang had grown up because of the machinations of the treacherous Thigiru. What was left of the gang moved to a safer area.

13

The 3rd (Kenya) Battalion of the Kings African Rifles takes over from the 4th (Uganda) Battalion

When the Malaya-jungle-experienced 3rd K.A.R. arrived back in Kenya to relieve the 4th K.A.R., their fine reputation preceded them. The 3rd KAR's record of successes against the tough communist terrorists was second to none. In eighteen months they had killed more bandits than any other unit that ever served there. Apart from their natural ability in the wilderness, they were well led by senior officers from British regiments who had volunteered to serve with African troops in action in a foreign field. Several officers had agreed to demotion in order to take command of companies. All company commanders, normally Majors, were actually Colonels.

The Regiment was commanded by Col. Joe Crewe-Read, tall, slightly stooped with a large aquiline nose, giving him a vulturine appearance. He was a popular leader. But with such seniority under his command, his job became almost entirely administrative. He was particularly able in this function. The job of organizing patrols against the bandits was left to the experienced, senior company commanders. But, in order to make his presence felt, Joe insisted that all his officers learn Swahili. This was not a popular order, but though the officers who were to serve only a two year term in the battalion, they acquiesced with good humor.

So effective were the 3rd K.A.R. in their actions in Malaya, that when they were recalled to Kenya on the declaration of the Mau-Mau Emergency, a big farewell parade was organized. The Commander-in-Chief of British forces in Malaya, General Sir Gerald Templar, was to take the salute. Senior officers from the Colonial Service and the Police were to attend, along with other senior military officers.

The chief Colonial Administration Officer had served in Kenya in a senior position, and had been to Jeans School in Nairobi. This was an academy where officers serving in colonial administration and military units in Kenya attended courses, including Swahili lessons. The standards were very high, and anyone aiming to pass the Swahili examinations had to be well acquainted with the language. So, the first speech made by the ex-Kenya senior Administration Officer at the farewell parade was in very correct, flowing Swahili. This was followed by the Commissioner of Police who had also served in Kenya, and also knew the language well. His Swahili was equally correct.

General Sir Gerald Templar now had to make his speech, but of course he didn't speak Swahili. Knowing of Joe Crew-Read's insistence that his officers learn the language, he turned to Joe and asked him to translate for him. The tall, vulturine figure of Joe rose nervously to his feet. Unfortunately, he had failed to give himself the order to learn the language, so his Swahili was barely of the 'kitchen' variety, as used by European housewives in Kenya.

The General's highly rhetorical speech ended with words along the following lines:- "And by your resolution and successes you have provided an example that has raised the determination and morale, not only of all the other troops serving here, but also of the gallant administration officers and the brave police."

Joe's translation fell a little short:- "*Na Bwana General*

anasema mzuri sana." (And the General says very good.) This was very well received as it cut the blah to a minimum, a point always popular with soldiers.

The Swahili word *Bwana* has several meanings. Basically it is a word of respect, and in the context of the above, there is really no equivalent in English. In modern times it has come to mean Mr., Sir; master (boss), but it also has the connotation of worthy personage. Another form of address is *Mzee* which has a similar sense of respect. Literally *Mzee* means old person, but has connotations of dignitary, elder or sage - wise one, and is more frequently used when addressing an older person.

Neither *Bwana* nor *Mzee* reflect subservience in the person using the term. That is to say they do not imply 'Oh Lord and Master', as many Europeans suppose when they first arrive in Kenya. A person holding a superior position may well use either term when addressing a person of lower rank or social status for whom he has respect.

* * *

The battle-hardened troops of the 3rd KAR and their British officers were back in Africa. They did not know what to expect from the Kenya Regiment soldiers. Unwarranted assumptions were easily made. The sons of settlers were assumed to be overly privileged, difficult to discipline, idle, African-hating louts. Reports from battalion headquarters indicated that as soon as the new arrivals were familiar with the territory, the services of the European Kenya Regiment sergeants would no longer be necessary. Meanwhile, the British army was in a quandary. In Malaya, African Warrant Officer Patrol Commanders (WOPCs), who in British regiments would have been commissioned officers, were to be under command of Kenya Regiment sergeants.

At one time there had been a rank in some K.A.R. battalions equal to 2nd Lieutenant. But the *Efendi* rank had been discontinued. Now a problem arose. If the WOPCs were commissioned, they would suffer a reduction in pay, as warrant officers enjoy higher rates of pay than junior commissioned officers. Furthermore, promotion to commissioned rank would affect the whole of the K.A.R., and other African forces throughout the British colonies in Africa. So, the Kenya Regiment Sergeants had to be commissioned. However, the cost of the officers mess bills, including standard charges, would exceed the pay we would earn as junior officers, and we decided to decline the promotion. Finally a solution was determined. The mandatory contributions to the Regimental Band Fund, the Regimental Silver Fund and other regimental funds were waived and we were commissioned.

While we understood the jungle-experienced troops were damn good, so were we. We thought we might also be required to stiffen morale, as the 3rd K.A.R., being a Kenya battalion, was to be in action against Kenya Africans. Our new company commanders had served as second-in-command of the companies in Malaya. They were experienced in jungle warfare, and in the handling of African soldiers. Like the Colonel, they regarded us with a jaundiced eye. They were embarrassed by our rank of sergeant, but were prepared to put up with us for a short time during which the capable WOPCs would become familiar with the area in which they were to operate.

We began to hunt down terrorists without being seen or heard. Mau-Mau casualties rose without loss to our patrols, and our officers gained a new-found and solid respect for our abilities.

Even prior to promotion to officer rank, I had been accepted by my men, who followed my leadership without question. Perhaps the mantle of command fell too easily on the shoulders of the sons of colonialists, and was accepted too easily by African soldiers. I was most fortunate and privileged to serve with the 3rd KAR, the finest jungle fighters anywhere.

When the Kenya Regiment personnel who had been serving with the 4th K.A.R. were transferred to the 3rd K.A.R., I was posted to C. Company which was commanded by Major Roy Stockwell. He had served with the battalion for several years and had a wealth of yarns to relate.

One of Roy Stockwell's stories about the 3rd Battalion of the K.A.R. when operating against communist terrorists in the Malayan jungle is worth repeating. To arrive in terrorist country, a long, tiring struggle through dense jungle was necessary. This took up to a week, and a patrol had to be provisioned by air drops. This activity gave the enemy a good idea that a patrol was entering the area, and the bandits would quietly withdraw. It was decided to try parachuting patrols into bandit controlled areas, thereby ensuring that the patrols would be fresh and fully provisioned when they were most likely to hit terrorist gangs. The idea was explained to the African patrol commanders.

"You will be dropped from a hovering helicopter from 700 feet into a clearing with supplies for the first few days. This will mean that you will not have to slog through the jungle for a week to get to the bandit inhabited area." The briefing officer smiled encouragingly at the squad, who had listened to the new idea intently. "Any questions?" he asked.

An African Warrant Officer Patrol Commander (WOPC) rose to his feet and asked. "Sir, would it not be better if we were to be dropped from a lower altitude, say 400 feet?"

"Ah!" said the briefing officer. "You are worried about the enemy seeing you during the drop. But the height from which you will be dropped is determined by the time it takes parachutes to open. If you were to be dropped from 400 feet, the parachutes would not have time to open."

"Oh, you didn't say we are to drop by parachute," said the W.O.P.C.

14

Treatment in a British Military Hospital, Nairobi

From about the age of eight, I had suffered from severe migraine attacks resulting in blinding headaches and disturbed vision. Loss of vision started with a bright swirling spot which expanded over a period of about half an hour until I was totally 'blind' but for random swirling patterns. Then the headache started. I lost the power of speech, my fingertips became numb, and eventually I became semi-conscious. A bad attack would last up to three days.

Then in 1954, when I was serving with the 3rd K.A.R., I suffered an attack which was to last sixteen days. The day the attack started, the Battalion Medical Officer visited our Company HQ. He came to my tent, and questioned me for nearly an hour. Then he sent me to the British Military Hospital in Nairobi in a Land Rover with my platoon Sergeant, and several pages of handwritten notes. I was admitted, taken to a ward, and put to bed. Although not fully aware of what was going on around me, I did wonder why my sergeant was advised not to hang my beret above my bed, lest the African male orderlies see that I was a Kenya Regiment soldier.

Every day the Chief Medical Officer (C.M.O.) came

round the wards with members of the medical staff. All patients were required to lie on their backs with their arms to their sides in a position of attention. Nurses hurried round to ensure that not only were the patients looking neat and tidy, but the beds were well turned out too. The patient was expected to lie without moving - without breathing would have been preferable - until the C.M.O. with his retinue had completed his round of the ward.

Being in unbearable pain, all I wanted to do was curl up in a fetal position. I wished I were dead. Each day the C.M.O. asked me if the medication was making me better, and each day I told him I was getting no medication. "The poor lad doesn't know what's going on," Matron claimed, and I'd be left to suffer in silence.

One day I was taken to a small room for a lumbar puncture. I am sure it was a demonstration, as the C.M.O. gave a running commentary on what he was doing. I didn't need to know he was about to jab a great needle into my spine, and if he hit the spinal cord, I'd be better off dead. But I was gratified to learn that the fluid being drawn off was clear. This, apparently, meant I was not suffering from tertiary syphilis.

After the lumbar puncture had been administered, I was left on the bed. The room had two doors, and a cold breeze swept through making me feel a mite more miserable. I had been dressed in one of those dreadfully embarrassing gowns that open down the back, and which the nurses never tie to keep one's rear view private and confidential. My rear view became particularly cold, and eventually I got off the bed, and blindly felt my way back to my ward.

On my arrival, a couple of my comrades-in-distress helped me to my bed. Some time later Matron came bustling in.

"Where have you been? I've been looking for you everywhere. Where have you been? How did you get back here? Who brought you here?"

"I…"

"Who told you to come back here?"

"I…"

"I've been looking for you everywhere. Where have you been?"

"I came back on my own. I…"

"Who said you could? You had no right to get up and come back here."

"Well, I was just lying there and getting pretty cold, so I…"

"You were supposed to stay there until I came back."

"Nobody told me that. I was left…"

"Don't you know it's dangerous to walk about after a lumbar puncture?"

"No. Nobody told me that."

"You could have damaged your brain. The fluid in which your brain floats had been drawn off. You could have bruised your brain. You could have done permanent damage."

"I haven't got a brain," I blurted angrily, "If I had a brain, it was addled by the sun when I was a child."

"Don't be silly," retorted Matron.

"Anyway, I don't care. I just want to die."

"Don't be silly. The medicine the doctor's prescribed will soon make you better." I thought I detected a faint tone of concession in Matron's last remark.

"I am NOT getting any medicine," I said emphatically with vigor.

"Of course you are…."

"I am NOT."

"You are. You just don't…."

"I am NOT. Oh, go away!" I shouted rudely. I'd had enough. I was in pain and was not prepared to argue with Matron. I turned on my side and pulled the blanket over my head in a gesture of dismissal.

"You must promise me you'll never do such a thing again. Getting up and walking after a lumbar puncture is very dangerous…………I'm waiting for your promise."

The room seemed to spin as I sat up, "I promise I'll never get up too soon after a lumbar puncture again. Now, for the love of Heaven, leave me to die in peace."

"Don't be silly. The medicine will soon have you well……..."

"Oh! Go away," I moaned in anguish. Was there nothing I could do to rid myself of this silly woman?

"Humph!" exploded matron who, at last, turned on her heel and left. Clearly, in her opinion, I was not grateful for all the attention I was getting. I was a surly, uncivil boor.

The farce continued. Daily Matron leaned over me.

"And how are we today?" she asked sweetly, "Is the medication helping us?" She gushed. I became a tad testy.

"I don't know about you but I am not well. I am NOT, NOT, NOT getting any medicine. Look, my mother, who was a nurse, lives two hundred yards away. Give me the pills. Let me go home. Mum will see that I take the damn medicine. I am NOT getting any medicine here. I am NOT getting better here. I am going to DIE here."

I think the hospital authorities were getting bored with me, so I was taken to the dispensary, given a box of tablets - normally given only to pregnant women, according to the dispenser - and escorted home. Mum was a bit shaken when she saw me being led to the house by a European nurse, but soon had me in bed with a tablet to assist me in my 'pregnancy'.

In two days, after finally receiving medication, I was better, and managed to get a lift back to Battalion HQ, and from there to my company. The episode had angered me. I asked the Company Commander if I could go on patrol. I'd had eighteen days off, lounging in Nairobi while my comrades had been patrolling the forest. My request was granted, and before dawn the following morning I set off with seven of my men.

We advanced three miles through the forest into the bamboo belt. Suddenly I felt the urge to order my team into line abreast, instead of in file, and to fix bayonets. I have no idea what induced me to give those orders. No sooner had we begun to advance again, than I saw a lone terrorist walking fifty yards away across our line of advance. I signaled to my team, most of whom had seen the man. I raised my rifle but was reluctant to shoot, and possibly alert his camp. But the man saw me. He jerked to a halt. I shot him. The bullet hit his hand, and carried some of his metacarpal bones into his belly. It was a ghastly wound, but I was not able to attend to the poor wretch immediately.

We charged past him, through the bamboo, and found ourselves at the top of a shallow valley, at the bottom of which was a Mau-Mau camp. There were several lean-tos, and about a dozen men stood in a line at the head of which three terrorists were attending to them. Another dozen gang members sat in groups of four or five around small fires. Amazingly, they hadn't heard my shot. Perhaps the bamboo deadened the sound, or maybe it was because the sound had gone over their heads, as they were down in the valley.

Now they saw us. There was no going back. We were committed. We had to rely on our training and fire power. The eight of us charged down on a gang three times our number. *Choma! Choma! Choma!* (Stab! Stab! Stab!) we screamed, hoping to scare the living daylights out of them with our bayonets. In a flash they dispersed, took cover, and opened fire on us. They had automatic weapons, a Bren, two Sten sub-machine guns as well as rifles. We took cover, and searched for targets.

I spotted a man in an army greatcoat, and carefully and deliberately began to fire at him. While I was concentrating on this, I was hit on the head. I was quite surprised how little it hurt. Then I realised that a 4 inch diameter bamboo stem by my shoulder had been cut through by automatic fire from the enemy. The twenty-five foot long bamboo had fallen across my head. I put the last few shots from my magazine into the target as my men fired at any enemy movement. On my orders, we charged down into the terrorists' camp. *Choma! Choma! Choma!*

I bayoneted the man in the greatcoat only to discover there was nobody in it. I now had a badly holed ex-military greatcoat. We raced across the river, but the gang had split up, and had run off in many directions. My men and I regrouped in the Mau-Mau camp. I hastened to attend to the wounded terrorist. There was nothing I could do other than to fill him up with morphine. He died as I did this. We collected the dead, and searched the camp. Two terrorists were found hiding under bushes overhanging the river. They were lying on their backs with only their faces above the icy water. We took them prisoner.

We found two sacks near a lean-to. They were both full of vials of yellow powder, and the vials were marked 'B.M.H. (British Military Hospital) Nairobi'. The prisoners told us they had been in line to receive an injection when we attacked them. We dragged the bodies of the dead away from the river, removed their documents, cut up their clothing, and destroyed the camp. I contacted company headquarters by radio. After speaking to the Company Commander, we hurried back to Company H.Q. with our prisoners and the sacks of B.M.H. drugs.

On our arrival the first person I bumped into was none other than the Battalion Medical Officer who was paying one of his routine visits to our Company.

"What the hell are you doing here? You're supposed to be in the UK!" he cried.

I picked up the two sacks of vials, and we went into the Company Office where I told him and the Company Commander my story. The M.O. took notes, and told me the letter he had given me to hand to the doctors at the B.M.H. had recommended I be sent to the UK for treatment.

Taking the two sacks with him, the M.O. got into his Land Rover, and raced off in a cloud of dust. We heard later he had driven straight to the B.M.H., and demanded to see the Chief Medical Officer who, he was told, was attending a meeting. He barged into the meeting, dumped the two sacks on the table, and demanded to know how two sacks of sulfa drugs marked 'B.M.H. Nairobi' had gotten into a Mau-Mau camp. Forty-eight hours later, the C.M.O. was out of Kenya.

We later heard he had been sent out to take charge of the B.M.H. in Nairobi to rid England of him. He had been responsible for an incident at a military hospital in the UK. On his round of the wards, the Medical Officer had insisted a delirious patient was faking, and ordered nurses not to attend to him. Moments later the thrashing man fell off the bed and died.

Investigations later revealed that virtually all the African dressers (orderlies) employed at the B.M.H. had taken Mau-Mau oaths. A man suffering from acute constipation, and another suffering from acute diarrhea had their medicines swapped. The man with acute diarrhea nearly died of dehydration. He had to be held on the toilet by some of the other patients. The man with constipation appeared about twelve months pregnant before matters were put right.

I wondered if the British doctors and senior nursing staff were also sympathetic towards the terrorists. No doubt the medication I was supposed to have been taking, had been stolen. Security of drugs was evidently non-existent. I was in a ward of twenty patients, only three of whom had been diagnosed, and they had been diagnosed in Korea before coming to Kenya.

**

My migraine illness was probably due to my having spent most of a period of three months in the forests of the Aberdare Range, sleeping in the open, and on an inadequate diet. Over a period of a little more than three months I spent almost ninety days in the forest, losing nearly seventy pounds from my fighting weight of two hundred and seven pounds. We had two breaks, each of a week or so, to replace equipment, replenish ammunition, launder our clothes, wash our dirty bodies and have our hair cut.

Back at company base, I quickly put back the weight I lost when in the forest. I ate the same forest rations as my African soldiers, but they did better than I on the diet of rice and canned corned beef. The men were also issued with ghee (clarified butter), tea, sugar and condensed milk.

The rice was supposed to be boiled in mess tins, but the tins were too small to cook a man's full day's ration of rice. We had to boil the rice ration for several men in a large, heavy steel dixie which, of course, had to be carried into the forest. When the rice was cooked, ghee was added, together with crumbled corn beef. (Six ounces per man per day). I took canned butter in place of the bitter tasting ghee.

We supplemented our rations with young stinging nettles which did much to ward off the effects of an inadequate diet. Nettles make a reasonably drinkable soup which has a slightly tart taste. We added nettles to the rice when it was being boiled. Water came from the streams running down from high up on the mountains. This water was potable without the addition of the chlorine tablets that were issued to sterilize water. We boiled water for tea, but otherwise drank it untreated with no ill effects.

Hardtack rations palled. We could carry eight days rations, but then relied on air drops by the Kenya Police Air Wing. When these air drops were delayed, we had to live off the land. Bushbuck were fairly plentiful, but one had to be lucky to see a bushbuck before it ran off.

Shooting warned the terrorists, and large game such as buffalo, rhino and elephant might well be startled and run. They would usually run off in the direction they happened to be facing and, if that was in your direction, you might have a herd of scared elephants or buffalo or a rhino charging through the patrol. So, shooting for the pot was avoided.

Frequently we went hungry, and our misery was exacerbated by the high altitude we endured in the mountains. This, together with the cold, wet nights, led to edema amongst my men. Many men developed coughs due to the high altitude, weather conditions and from the smoke of camp fires. A man afflicted with a cough couldn't be taken on patrol as coughing would warn the enemy of our approach. If one of my soldiers started to cough, he had to be taken back to platoon HQ, as he wouldn't get better until he got back to a lower altitude, to a warm, dry tent, and received medical treatment. In the period of just under three months, sickness reduced my platoon from twenty-eight to eight, including myself.

We sometimes heard the enemy cough. They tried to cure coughs by taking doses of Doctor Sloan's liniment which was supposed to relieve stiff and sore muscles. This was a fiery treatment, and its effects on the digestive system must have been disastrous.

Casualties among the terrorists from our activities and from sickness were so high, they moved away from our area of the forest. Patrolling became a boring chore with very few encounters with the enemy. We were moved down to a lower, warmer, drier area in the Kikuyu Reserve where we regained our health. My platoon was soon up to full strength.

Moving a company of K.A.R. soldiers required about 20% of the number of trucks required to move a company of British troops. The K.A.R. had fewer tents, smaller and lighter camp beds, less rations and clothing and fewer personal effects. And the K.A.R patrols were far more mobile in the forest. The British Army twenty-four hour ration-pack was heavy and bulky. It contained high calorie items which I found nauseating. Supplying a K.A.R. patrol by air-drop was relatively simple. A sack containing enough rations for eight men for eight days could be dropped in one pass by a light aircraft. Sufficient rations for eight days for eight British soldiers, was a much larger exercise.

The KAR's mobility was a major advantage when operating patrols in the forests.

15

3rd K.A.R. takes over Fort Essex

When the 3rd K.A.R. took over the area that had been controlled by the 4th KAR, Fort Essex, deep in the forest of the Abedare Range continued to be used. It had proved to be an effective base from which to patrol. Other army units followed our lead, and also built permanent camps high up in the forest.

One day when my platoon was occupying Fort Essex, a herd of ten elephants, intrigued by our buildings, came to inspect our efforts. They walked slowly past our camp, within ten paces of the perimeter defenses. They appeared to be completely unperturbed by our presence, and seemed quite tame as they strolled past. There are Africans who have never seen an elephants, and although we had come across these wonderful animals in the forest from time to time, they were always partially hidden by trees and undergrowth.

Now we could see the whole herd clearly, and I was worried when one of my Turkana soldiers, Lokkitulia, suddenly raced towards them, yelling at the top of his voice. He had removed the magazine from his Patchett and was waving his arms above his head with the magazine in one hand and the Patchett in the other, showing us that he had no intention of shooting at the herd. The elephants eyed him calmly, and made off into the forest with barely any increase in their pace. Lokkitulia watched them go, turned and walked back to where the whole platoon was now gathered.

"There you are," he said. "They're just like cattle. They're not dangerous. Who said they are dangerous? They're just like big cows!"

I was exasperated, as it did seem that the herd had been unconcerned by Lokkitulia's maniacal yelling. I stood spluttering, wondering what had gotten into the man, and how I was going to reprimand him. Obviously the elephants would not have been able to charge us unless they had found the gateway open, but it is not a wise thing to upset an elephant herd in any way, particularly when there are youngsters present, as there were on this occasion.

Two or three Turkana soldiers took the offender to one side, and relieved me of the necessity to remonstrate. Lokkitulia had been foolish, and his tribal comrades were quite capable of teaching him a lesson not to bring derision down on the whole Turkana tribe. Clearly, they told him, even the elephants now thought that the Turkana were silly fellows.

***

Roy Stockwell told me that some seven years earlier, the 3rd KAR traveled by train from Nanyuki to Mombasa. It was a long, uncomfortable, two day journey, and the soldiers were unable to get much sleep sitting upright on slatted wooden benches. Arriving at Mombasa at about 8.00 a.m., the Battalion was formed into three ranks, and marched out of the railway station to begin a 25 mile route march to a deserted site on the coast south of Mombasa.

They arrived at the location in the evening, and set about making camp. Earlier, their tents, bedding and rations

LOKITULIA IN TURKANA TRIBAL DRESS WITH KINSMEN.

had been brought by trucks. The camp was within 150 ft. of the beach, but the men were so weary that, after setting up their tents, and eating a satisfying meal, they fell into bed after a cursory glance at the sea, which was at full high tide.

The following morning the men completed camp duties after breakfast. Still wearied by their long train journey and 25 mile march, the men were given the rest of the day to recover. Lokkitulia strolled down to the white sandy beach. There he began to wander up and down the strand, apparently searching for something. Roy Stockwell watched the soldier for a few minutes before being overcome by curiosity. What was the man searching for? Unable to contain his inquisitiveness any longer, he went down to the beach to ask Lokkitulia, "What are you looking for?"

"Cattle tracks," was the terse reply.

"Cattle? What cattle?" asked Roy.

"The cattle that came during the night, Sir." Lokkitulia sighed with impatience. Didn't Europeans know anything about cattle?

"There were no cattle here during the night," said Roy.

"There certainly were, Sir. Many cattle. Why else did the water go down so far?" asked Lokkitulia pointing to the sea, now at low tide.

"Go down to the water, dip your hand in and taste it," suggested Roy.

Lokkitulia complied.

"*Kumbe! Maji ya chumvi.* (Wow! Salt water.)"

Like many from semi-arid areas, Lokkitulia had never seen so much water before, and didn't know he was looking at a tidal ocean.

***

I have often wondered why some men, in the heat of battle, are more effective soldiers than others. One answer may be that bright and alert soldiers become overexcited when bullets start flying about. More stolid men are roused by the excitement to become highly effective. Lokkitulia was one of the latter. He spent most of his waking hours daydreaming about his cattle back home. How many calves had been born? Had his family had to move to better grazing grounds? Was his old favorite cow still alive and giving milk? Lokkitulia was frequently absorbed in such thoughts. But he was brave and lethal in battle. He had been awarded the Distinguished Service Medal for courageous action in Malaya.

I was happy to have Lokkitulia in my platoon. He had shown exceptional fighting spirit on more than one occasion. But he was rather gormless (lacking initiative) when there was no danger to excite him.

Lokkitulia learns a lesson

Maj. Roy Stockwell was well loved by all the men in his company. He was surprisingly fit and had unusual stamina. Eighteen months earlier in Malaya, at the age of forty-five, he had won a mile race against all comers. At that time there were many very fit, young soldiers serving in Malaya. In our company headquarters in Kenya, Roy became bored with administration chores, and decided that he needed exercise. He told me he wanted to accompany my tracker team on our next patrol into the forest.

I insisted he command the team as he was the senior officer, and I was not prepared for him to be merely an observer. Roy demurred but eventually acquiesced. I wanted Roy to experience the onerous responsibilities of a tracker team commander in action should we run into a Mau-Mau gang. I also wanted him to experience the difficult task of map reading in the forest when it was nearly impossible to determine, with any accuracy, a patrol's position.

We set off for the forest in pre-dawn darkness, and as soon as we were amongst the trees, Roy ordered our advance

MAJOR ROY STOCKWELL.

parallel to the edge of the forest. He had decided we were to cross a deep river valley. It was raining heavily, and we climbed down the steep valley, slipping and sliding all the way. We crossed the ice cold stream, and proceeded to clamber up the other side of the valley. We were carrying full packs, theoretically weighing forty-five pounds, but with a few extras, they weighed quite a bit more. It took us four and a half hours to cross the valley. We had to struggle with heavy packs and our weapons up the steep, slippery slope.

When Roy halted and looked back to see how the rest of us were getting on, I signaled to him that we needed to rest. I told him I thought we were nearing the top of the ridge. It was possible the Mau-Mau, had they heard or seen us coming and may have set up an ambush knowing we would be exhausted from our noisy climb and ill-prepared for action.

Roy signaled to the team that we were to rest for twenty minutes. He found a convenient rock to sit on, and Lokkitulia sat down beside him. After a few minutes, Lokkitulia looked at Roy with an amused glint in his eyes, and heaved an exaggerated sigh.

"W-h-a-t?" asked Roy.

"I suppose someone will have to carry your pack for you when we get to the top," Lokkitulia answered. He heaved another great sigh. "I suppose it will be me".

Very quietly and slowly Roy said, "If you don't get to the top before me, you WILL carry my pack!"

And with that, Roy leapt to his feet, and went up the slope like a demented jackrabbit with Lokkitulia scuttling after him in hot pursuit. All thoughts of a possible ambush had been forgotten by Roy and Lokkitulia. The rest of us were obliged to scramble after them as fast as we could, hoping if there was an ambush, we might still be able to save the lives of our two crazy comrades. There was no ambush, and Lokkitulia did have to carry Roy's pack - for fifteen minutes or so, before Roy relieved him of it with a huge smile.

"Huh!" he said with satisfaction, "You think this *mzee* (old man) can't keep up with you idle, degenerate, clumsy soldiers?"

"No, SIR!" replied the chastened Lokkitulia.

A visitor comes to Fort Essex

One evening we had a radio call from an officer at Nakuru saying he was leaving to come to Fort Essex. It was raining hard and we calculated he would enter the forest at around 1.00 a.m. in the morning. So we tried to deter him as, although we considered the track to be 'all weather', in very heavy rain it was all too easy to slide off the track into thick mud. But the officer insisted, as an exceptionally skillful rally driver, he would be able to get through in an American WWII Willys Jeep.

We pointed out he would be passing through Mau-Mau country, and we could not protect him should his Jeep slide off the track and become bogged down. He brushed aside our objections, and said he was leaving Nakuru, and would see us at about 2.00 a.m. He had a circuitous route to negotiate along muddy, earth roads, in rain, at night. He would appreciate it if we could arrange to have a hot mug of coffee ready for his arrival.

We warned the guard commander, and put a man on the radio to receive messages. We then put down a barrage of 3 inch mortar fire 500 yards down the trail in a rather futile effort to deter any Mau-Mau from taking up ambush positions along the nine mile forest track. We then retired, fully clothed, with our boots on. At about 1.30 a.m. a message was received on the radio to advise us our intrepid visitor was about to enter the forest. He added the comment that it was raining rather hard. This we knew. It was pouring. Two hours later he informed us by radio that he was stuck someplace down the track. His jeep was belly down in nine inches of thick mud.

Six of us, including a giant whom we called K-K-

Kosmos due to a severe stutter, got into a Land Rover, and headed off down the track in pouring cold, cold rain. We had only gone about a mile when we came upon our now very unpopular visitor, Major Morgan. We had to turn our vehicle around to face the opposite direction. In the darkness and rain, we managed to get our Land Rover stuck belly down in the mud too. But we had Kosmos.

After ten minutes of trying ineffectually to push our Land Rover onto firmer ground, Kosmos peremptorily waved us aside, grasped the two handholds on the back of the Land Rover, picked up the back end of the vehicle out of nine inches of mud, and moved it sideways, in a series of lifts, onto the top of the camber and harder ground. I had never seen such a feat, but Kosmos thought nothing of it. We were now able to maneuver the Land Rover back down to the Jeep, hitch the two vehicles together with rope, and haul/push them up the track to a place where they stood on level, hard ground.

I turned to our unwanted, unloved visitor. "I'd remind you we spend our days hunting down Mau-Mau. Yesterday we battled a gang after we'd sneaked through thick bush to get round behind them onto a mound which gave us a clear view of their camp. It took us three hours of crawling, wriggling and snaking our way to get into position. We were successful, and managed to kill several Mau-Mau. Today we will go out to do battle again. We need our sleep. We do NOT need to spend the night hauling a mad major out of the mud, SIR."

"Terribly sorry old boy," murmured Major Morgan. "Got stuck, you see."

"Yeah. We know that." I was laconic. I turned and climbed into the mud splattered Land Rover. Not long after, we reached our camp to receive demands from Maj. Morgan for, not only a mug of hot coffee, but a hot bath too. We told him brusquely what he could do.

It turned out that he was a training officer, and had come out from England about a year ago. He had visions of becoming a rally driver, and wanted to experience driving in the mountains. He loved Jeeps. We pointed out that the all-steel Jeep was heavier than the aluminum-bodied Land Rover, and sank further in mud. He argued that our Land Rover had also become stuck.

"Ah!" we said, "but we have K-K-Kosmos as part of our Land Rover kit. He would never have been able to pick up a heavy Jeep," we opined.

Maj. Morgan demanded we get Kosmos out of his warm sleeping bag, take him out into the cold rain, and ask him to try to lift the Jeep. We told our visitor in British Army language to "Go forth and multiply!" We left Maj. Morgan sitting very wet and disconsolate on a camp chair while we snuggled down in our sleeping bags.

The following morning, he made copious notes and sketches of our camp, and the bamboo we had cut and prepared as building elements. I suspected that the would-be-rally-driver also made notes about his heroic struggle through rain, mud and darkness driving his beloved Jeep. I wondered if our advice about the advantages of the Land Rover were entered in his notes. After the rain stopped, he left amid our curt but heartfelt thanks. We never heard of him again.

16

Some Tribal Traits

Kikuyu tribesmen had never been recruited into the K.A.R. because of their alleged lack of moral fibre and reputation for treachery. The warrior tribes were expected to make good soldiers, although the Masai were excluded because of their isolationist attitudes, indolence and their unique diet of blood and milk. Their sister tribe, the Samburu, were however recruited, as were other warrior tribesmen from the Nandi group and the Turkana.

The Kamba hunter tribesmen were also considered potentially good soldiers, although they were deemed to be a cousin tribe of the Kikuyu with a similar language. Most of the tribe would deny this hotly. My own observations were that the Kamba are intelligent, clever soldiers with a high level of manual skill. They are of a humorous, cheerful disposition and are reliable.

The Nandi group provided courageous soldiers with considerable determination and zeal. They had a proud military tradition, and turned their hand to any form of farming, unlike their traditional enemies, the Masai, who only herded cattle. The Masai isolated themselves by their reluctance to engage in a wide range of activities - commerce, education, medicine and many other activities they considered to be beneath the dignity of warriors.

Since Kenya gained Independence, the Masai have had to change attitudes, and have joined in nation building. Perhaps, during colonial times, they were regarded as noble savages, and would not deign to engage in mundane activities. But after Independence, the rest of the nation may have told them to get up off their rumps and get on with it.

The Samburu and Turkana tribesmen in the army were regarded as somewhat less sophisticated than their comrades. The Samburu were alleged to take a herbal drug to enhance their courage, and it is possible that a permanent effect was to make them very excitable and unreliable, particularly in action when bullets began to fly around. Unlike the Samburu, the Turkana, who might seem slow on the uptake in normal times, became highly effective when excitement raised their level of efficiency.

It was said of the Turkana that nobody really knew from whence they had originated. It seemed that the tribe was slowly migrating, over decades, to the south, possibly from some place in Ethiopia or the Sudan. They had reached their present tribal area when the British colonial administration stopped further migration. It was further said of them that, had they met up with any of the other warrior tribes like the Masai or the Zulu of South Africa, they would have beaten them in battle without difficulty, as the Turkana were considered to be the most warlike tribe in Africa.

The Somali and related tribesmen were also considered potentially fine soldiers and the Somalis, in particular, considered themselves to be more cultured and intelligent, perhaps because they were not pagans, as was the case of the other tribesmen. In my experience, the Somalis may well be more cultured and intelligent, but I found that their loyalty was suspect. Not that they tended to side with the Mau-Mau, but they seemed to expect special treatment and, if they were not granted such treatment, withheld their loyalty.

However, I have to say that one of the best soldiers I ever met was a Somali, Abduraman, who rose to senior rank after Independence when Africans were commissioned as officers. He was truly a fine man and, though slight of build and of medium height, was endowed with that special something which commands instant respect. Abduraman was a Muslim who obtained good spiritual guidance from his religion. Being a Muslim, he didn't drink alcoholic beverages, the bane of so many soldiers.

Overindulgence

As with other native cultures all over the world, all too many Africans are destroyed by booze, which has become too conveniently available. In times of old, women brewed native 'pombe' (moonshine) between each full moon, when great parties were held. In between these booze-ups, little or no 'pombe' was available, and there was virtually no alcoholism. It is the availability of relatively cheap beer and lager that has resulted in the spread of alcoholism throughout Africa. President Kenneth Kaunda, the first president of Zambia, threatened to resign if the Zambians didn't mend their ways and restrict their drinking of alcoholic beverages.

A friend of mine, stationed in Zambia in the 70s, had arranged a short flight in a light aircraft together with two business colleagues. Bob arrived early at the airfield, and one of his colleagues arrived after a few minutes. His pal suggested they went to the lounge to share a bottle of beer. As they approached the building, five Zambian ladies entered the bar ahead of the two businessmen. Each lady ordered a quart of Castle beer and a tot of gin. During the time it took Bob and his colleague to finish a pint each, the ladies had each downed five quarts of beer and five gin 'chasers'.

I once attended a public function where I offered to buy an African politician a drink, asking him to tell the barman what he wanted. He ordered a tumbler full of brandy and a double liqueur brandy 'chaser' in a separate glass. The drinks were tossed back immediately, and the politician looked at me questioningly, as if to ask if I'd like to treat him again. I suddenly saw someone across the room that I had to talk to, so I excused myself.

17

Gentlewoman of the Bush

It was fun to meet culturally 'unspoiled' Africans. By this I mean those who had very little or no contact with Europeans or the more 'sophisticated' Africans from urban areas. On one patrol in a Kikuyu farming area, we came upon an isolated valley at the bottom of which there was a collection of six huts. The valley was steep on three sides and one end ran down to an opening where a stream drained the valley. Over the river there was a bridge half a mile from the huts.

I lead my tracker team down the dry, slippery, grass slope to the huts and found them to be the home of a Kikuyu family. We were met by the friendly family members who were not apprehensive of our arrival, a patrol of armed soldiers from other tribes, led by a *mzungu* (white man). It was usual for our patrols to be regarded as trusted, benevolent, orderly troops.

Outside one hut, sitting on a mound in the sun, was an elderly woman covered in ragged blanket. She patted the grass in a gesture for me to sit beside her. In surprisingly good Swahili, she told me that she had been crippled since birth, and in her sixty years had never been out of the valley.

I was the first *mzungu* she had ever seen close up. She had seen a European driving a car over the bridge but it was too far away to have seen what he looked like. She assumed that he was the District Officer (D.O.). In her life, the D.O. was the supreme authority. While we chatted, she gazed up into my face and gently stroked my arm.

"*Atiriri munduwakwa,*" (Listen friend,) she said in Kikuyu before reverting to Swahili, "do all *wazungu* (white people) have blue eyes?" she asked.

"Well, not all. Some have brown and others have green eyes," I replied.

"Does the District Officer have blue eyes?" she asked.

"I don't know. I haven't met him." I answered. "What color hair has he?"

"I don't know. It is too far to see when he drives over that bridge, and he wears a hat." The old lady shrugged, and continued. "You have hair on your arms. Do all *wazungu* have hairy arms?"

"Well, not all, and most *wazungu* women don't have hairy arms or only very short fair hairs. But most *wazungu* men have hairy arms."

"*Wewe kabila gani?*" (What tribe are you?)

"We don't really have tribes like you, but I am an Englishman."

"Do all Englishmen have blue eyes, hairy arms and brown hair on their heads?" She was very interested in my blue eyes. She had never seen blue eyes before.

"Well, no. As I said some have brown or green eyes. Some have little or no hair on their arms, and some have black hair, some have fair hair and some have ginger hair."

"*Kumbe!*" (Wow!) was her comment. And she went on to ask me all sorts of other questions. She wasn't being nosy, just curious, and I was reluctant to leave her with unanswered questions. She wanted to know about *wazungu* tribal customs - she couldn't accept that the English are not a tribe.

"What tribe are you?" she asked.

"*Tuseme, ya haki, waingereza ni kabila.*" (Let us say, in fact, the English are a tribe.) "*Si, wana luga yao?*" (Don't they have their own language?)

"Well, other people speak English too."

"*Nani?*" (Who?)

"Americans."

"Aren't they English?

"Well, not really. They are a mixture. Some went to America from England but others went from other countries. Now they live in one country and call themselves Americans. And they speak a form of English."

"*Kumbe!*" (Huh!) "Don't they speak real English?"

I smiled. "Not really."

"*Sababu?*" (Why?)

"Well, they fought for their *uhuru* (freedom), and broke away from England. Now the English they speak is less elegant. Less refined."

"*Kumbe!* ("Wow!") Why did they want *uhuru?*"

"They didn't want to pay taxes."

She grinned. "*Eeeeh.*" (Aaaaah) I understand. Like us. Some of us didn't want to pay Hut Tax. Do Americans have to pay taxes now?"

"Yes. To their own government."

Her eyes sparkled with amusement. "*Kumbe!* (Goodness me!) Didn't they know everyone has to pay taxes? How would the *Serikali* (Government) pay their employees, for the army, schools, roads and the District Officer if there were no taxes? The Americans must be *kichwa maji* (simple minded) if they didn't realise they would have to pay taxes. *Kwa vyote.* (Anyway.) *Una mke?* (Do you have a wife?) *We maru?*" (Are you circumcised?) She asked in Kikuyu. Her questions were becoming rather personal.

Our free roaming conversation went on for two or three hours, and I found many of her questions difficult to answer briefly. By the time we had to leave, all her family and my tracker team were sitting around us, many of her questions and my answers were of intense interest to all. I was very reluctant to leave as I really liked the old lady who I found charming, shrewd and interesting. Her dark brown eyes flashed with intelligence and humor. I also found her to be receptive, and hungry for knowledge of the world beyond her isolated valley.

A few members of her family had been out of the valley, some to towns where they had worked and lived among the more sophisticated people of the world, and it was from them she had learned Swahili. She was completely illiterate, and like many intelligent illiterates, she had an exceptional memory. Her learning ability was wonderful, but being a woman and crippled, she was treated as a pariah cur.

Much of her life had been spent on the ground among the dogs, chickens, goats and crawling infants. She wore dirty rags, and little interest was taken in her by family members. A long conversation was, for her, a rare event indeed. Her chat with a *mzungu* had never happened before - and was unlikely to occur again. I wondered if her family would treat her differently after I left. As I reluctantly departed, we shook hands, and I pressed a few shillings into her gnarled fingers. I hoped I had kindled a spark of interest in her family for her, and I knew this visit would be remembered, and debated for many years. I told them I had enjoyed our chat immensely, and that she was a wise elder, and should be treated with respect and due deference. They agreed.

18

Teamwork generates telepathy

From Ngalu, my platoon tracker, I was to gain tremendous knowledge. How good a tracker was I before Ngalu began to teach me? I don't remember. I like to think that I must have shown some skill in the art, and he recognized a worthwhile student. He had incredible eyesight. I've known him to count the tiles on the roof of a house.

In the years I spent hunting Mau-Mau, I developed a very keen sense of smell. On several occasions this enabled us to surprise the enemy, or avoid bumping into big game. My carrying of my binoculars had also led to successes in finding evidence of terrorists without being seen. So, Ngalu readily gave me a few points in bushcraft, and he knew this was reciprocated by my considerable respect for his knowledge, especially in the art of tracking. He was, besides, a wonderful character with a great sense of humor. He had a sixth sense, and time and time again offered to carry the Bren just before we hit a gang.

Naronga, a Rendile tribesman from northern Kenya, usually carried the Bren. He was a strong man, and the weight of the Bren and its spare magazines presented no problem for him. But he was always willing to hand it over

Ngalu

and take Ngalu's Patchett for a rest.

The Bren is a good weapon when contact with the enemy is made, but it is heavy and cumbersome in the jungle. Ngalu seemed to use Naronga as his personal gun bearer.

Ngalu and Naronga were good pals, and remained so despite Ngalu's incessant ribbing. Naronga was not the brightest spark, and Ngalu's teasing only made Naronga grateful for the attention from the most gifted member of the platoon. When the bullets were flying about, Naronga would always seek out his pal to act as his bodyguard. Ngalu always kept near me as my personal bodyguard.

Between the three of us had we had a range of acute senses and useful skills: Ngalu's eyesight and tracking ability; Naronga's outstanding courage and ability with the Bren, and my sense of smell and burgeoning understanding of tracker skills. We formed a close-knit team. The more experience we gained as a team, the greater the development of the combination of sixth senses. We often saw, heard, smelled or spotted evidence of the enemy at the same moment. The necessity for communication between the three of us became redundant. The rest of the men became confident in our abilities, and thus became eager to prove their own efficacy.

I had become an experienced patrol commander, and with my platoon of African soldiers had several successes under our belts. Friendly banter in Swahili lubricated occasions of hardship and disappointment.

We faced further perils with confidence.

GLOSSARY

Swahili. (Properly Kiswahili). The *lingua franca* of East Africa. The language developed over several hundred years when Arab slavers dominated the area. There is no Swahili tribe. A *Mswahili* is a *Kiswahili* speaking person. *Waswahili* are *Kiswahili* speaking people. The language has origins in the those of the coastal tribes of East Africa and Zanzibar, and in Arabic, Persian and Turkish. It has also borrowed from English, Hindi, German and there are traces of Portuguese. Arab slavers from Oman, Egypt, Saudi Arabia, Persia, Jordan and Syria operated, in safety, from the islands of Zanzibar and Pemba off the coast of Tanzania.

Kiswahili has five vowels each of which has only one sound:

A as in c<u>a</u>r; *E* as in g<u>e</u>t; *I* as ee in kn<u>ee</u>; *O* as in f<u>o</u>r; *U* as oo in b<u>oo</u>k. Diphthongs of two vowels are pronounced by running the two vowel sounds together as in the following examples: *Nairobi; shauri; tao,; toa;*

Ch as in chicken. *Th* as in thick. *Dh* as th in there.

The penultimate syllable is always stressed. Kiswahili words employ suffixes and this alters the pronunciation:

M<u>e</u>sa - table. *Mes<u>a</u>ni* - on the table. *Ch<u>u</u>mba* - room. *Chumb<u>a</u>ni* - in the room.

Words borrowed from Arabic, English and other languages do not use suffixes:

Ndani ya motoka - in the motor car (NOT *motokani*)

To simplify I have omitted the prefixes *M* and *Wa* in front of the names of tribes: *Kikuyu* instead of *Mkikuyu* - a Kikuyu person or *Wakikuyu* - Kikuyu people.

My next book, "More Military Musings", takes us through the Mau-Mau Rebellion, a difficult and dangerous time for both the white settlers and the majority of the Kikuyu and other tribes who wanted no part of terrorist activities.

In the midst of war, I experienced moments of humor and the gentle sensitivity in the relationships formed both by accident and intent.

I hope you, the reader of this book, as well as "Rambunctious Reflections" and "Rollicking Recollections", will contact me with your comments and questions. I can be reached by e-mail at banner@rof.net or by mail at PO Box 2141, Glenwood Springs CO 81602, USA

Leonard J. Gill

About the Author

Born in Kenya, East Africa, of English parents in December 1930, Len lived there until 1989.

Even in a period of anti-Mau Mau Rebellion operations Len found sensitive and happy incidents among the hell of bloodshed and killing.

Africans dubbed him with the nickname *Mpenda raha* (he who enjoys a good time). Len insists that a shot-glass of humor helps the worries go down.

Len served with African troops. With them, Len matured in a way that enabled him to balance horror with humor.

Military Musings epitomizes Len's ability to relate with sensitivity and understanding his army adventures. He pulls no punches in tales of deadly serious conflict, but he mitigates these with merrier moments.

Len now lives in Glenwood Springs, Colorado with his wife, Kaye and Shih-tzu, Bandit.

About the Book

Entertaining tales of a Kenya Regiment soldier serving with the Kings African Rifles in anti-Mau-Mau terrorist operations. Amid the serious incidents, there are humorous and enchanting anecdotes of unforgettable characters.

The book covers the relationships Len had with his African troops and their experiences which led to mutual respect and comradeship.

Together they faced danger from terrorist ambushes, rogue animals and the cold, damp climate of high altitude and nutritionally inadequate diet.

Sensitive contacts with the civil population led to trust and friendship toward him and his soldiers.

ISBN 1553956540